RED FLAGS *AND* LACE COIFFES

RED FLAGS AND

LACE COIFFES

IDENTITY AND SURVIVAL IN A BRETON VILLAGE

CHARLES R. MENZIES

Teaching Culture: UTP Ethnographies for the Classroom

UNIVERSITY OF TORONTO PRESS

Library and Archives Canada Cataloguing in Publication

Menzies, Charles R.
   Red flags and lace coiffes : identity and survival in a Breton fishing village / Charles R. Menzies.

Includes bibliographical references and index.
ISBN 978-1-4426-0512-1

   1. Fishing villages—France—Bigouden. 2. Fishing villages—Economic aspects—France—Bigouden. 3. Fishing villages—Social aspects—France—Bigouden. 4. Fishers—Social life and customs—France—Bigouden. 5. Bretons—France—Bigouden—Social life and customs. I. Title.

DC611.B851M469 2011   944'.11084   C2011-902439-X

We welcome comments and suggestions regarding any aspect of our publications—please feel free to contact us at news@utphighereducation.com or visit our Internet site at www.utppublishing.com.

North America
5201 Dufferin Street
North York, Ontario, Canada, M3H 5T8

2250 Military Road
Tonawanda, New York, USA, 14150

ORDERS PHONE: 1-800-565-9523
ORDERS FAX: 1-800-221-9985
ORDERS E-MAIL: utpbooks@utpress.utoronto.ca

UK, Ireland, and continental Europe
NBN International
Estover Road, Plymouth, PL6 7PY, UK
ORDERS PHONE: 44 (0) 1752 202301
ORDERS FAX: 44 (0) 1752 202333
ORDERS E-MAIL: enquiries@nbninternational.com

The University of Toronto Press acknowledges the financial support for its publishing activities of the Government of Canada through the Canada Book Fund.

Printed in Canada

Portions of this book originally appeared:
• as "Class and Identity on the Margins of Industrial Society: A Breton Illustration," *Anthropologica* 39 (1997): 27–38, and are reproduced with the permission of the editors of that journal.
• as "Fishing, Families, and the Survival of Artisanal Boat-Ownership in the Bigouden Region of France," MAST (*Maritime Studies*) 2,1 (2003): 71–88. Used with permission.
• as "Chapter 17. Red Flags and Lace Coiffes: Identity, Livelihood, and the Politics of Survival in the Bigoudennie, France," in *Culture, Economy, Power: Anthropology as Critique, Anthropology as Praxis*, edited by Winnie Lem and Belinda Leach. State University of New York Press ©2002, State University of New York. All rights reserved.

All photographs are taken by the author except the following:
   Figures 0.1, 0.2 and 0.6 are courtesy of Veronica Ignas.
   Figures 0.7 and 7.1 are courtesy of Tristan Menzies.
   Figures 1.1, 1.3, and 2.4 are used with permission of Comité local des pêches maritimes du Guilvinec.
   Figure 2.1 is used with permission of Alain le Quernec.

To my parents, Shirley and Harry Basil Menzies,
to my partner and dear friend, Veronica Ignas, and
to my sons, Tristan and Jarek, without whom my
life would have been significantly impoverished.

CONTENTS

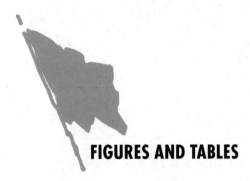

FIGURES AND TABLES

FIGURES

TABLES

PREFACE

THIS BOOK EMERGED OUT OF MY LIFELONG CONCERN with fisherfolk. These are people whose lives are governed by the rhythm of the ocean and the imposition of social policies and economic forces, which are at times beyond their immediate capacity to alter. This is a story of one small Breton fishing community's struggle to survive in the midst of constant crisis and external pressure. Anthropologists appreciate the differences that exist from place to place; hence our interest in studying the variation of human cultures. Stories of particular places can also help us make sense of wider social processes such as globalization. The global pressures that these Breton fisherfolk have faced are similar to those that members of other rural communities are facing even as they approach these social forces through the cultural and historical lenses of their own cultural particularism.

In this book I consider how social class, gender, and kinship are implicated in the struggle for survival. These are critical concepts in and for anthropology. Anthropology, in the abstract, is the study of human society in all its manifest diversity through time. The anthropological study of humanity is based in the day-to-day activities of people carrying on their lives. Anthropological archaeologists look to the ancient remains of human societies; they examine the traces left behind by human actions. Socio-cultural anthropologists, from the subfield of anthropology within which this book is written, are able to observe and speak with people as they are living their lives. As we do this, we draw on a core set of critical concepts and ideas to help make sense of the messiness of real life: social class, gender, and kinship.

Social class is more than simply a set of rankings based on occupation, income, or prestige. In explaining social class, I often compare a layer-cake model of class with the more useful relational model. A layer cake may consist of two, three, or more layers piled one on top of each other. The boundaries between each layer may or may not be easy to see depending upon the type of frosting one has used. Ultimately the real boundary between layers may be an arbitrary one. In this model, social classes are seen as layers piled one on top of the other; to distinguish between them, it is useful considering things such as differences in education or income. However, the layer-cake model of social class is not as helpful in a context such as a Breton fishport, where one's relation to the means of production—tools, boats, machinery— makes a crucial difference to how one understands and fits into the local society. The relational model of class considers how human labour is organized in terms of who owns what and who does what work. In this model, one focuses on the deployment of labour and the structure of ownership in the act of production. Who owns the boat? Who works on the boat? Social class is complicated and complemented (as we will see later on in this book) by gender and the organization of kinship.

The gendered roles that people play within a society are critical for understanding how a particular society works. Gender is the term that anthropologists and other social scientists use to identify the socially constructed roles assigned to men, women, or other genders as opposed to the biological category of sex, that is, female or male. Fishing communities share strongly demarcated gendered worlds of work and family. Men are almost universally the people who harvest fish. Women are engaged in shoreside activities. Both genders play a crucial role in the continuation of the fishing way of life.

Kinship—the way in which people reckon their connections through birth, adoption, and marriage—is a ubiquitous feature of human societies. Yet we have almost as many ways of determining kinship as we do peoples. There was a time when it might have been correct to say that anthropology was the study of kinship systems. This is no longer the case. However, the way in which people form families, share resources through these family networks, and construct systems of belonging and affect remains a critically important aspect of anthropological study today. It is clear that even in communities such as the Breton fishing community discussed in this book, kinship plays an important role in shaping people's ability to stay afloat in turbulent social and economic times.

Without the support and assistance of my family, this project would not have emerged as it did. My parents, Shirley and Harry Basil Menzies, have been unfailing in their support. In the years leading up to and during my fieldwork in France and throughout the writing and revisions of this book, I have benefited greatly from the detailed commentary of Veronica Ignas. Our sons, Jarek and Tristan, shared the fieldwork experience. They have had much to say about the process, and I have grown by listening to their attempts to make sense of my work as an anthropologist. To Jarek, Tristan, and Veronica and to my parents, Shirley and Basso, I offer a heartfelt thank you.

My friends Anthony Marcus and Kate McCaffrey read pages of early drafts. It has been a pleasure to grow wiser in their company (even if they are a world away). I would especially like to thank Gerald Sider for his challenging and inspiring commentary; his words have left a lasting impression on the way I see the world. Gerry has been a mentor and friend who shows through his actions that politically engaged and inspired writing is possible.

My special thanks to Jean-Jacques and Anne-Marie Coïc, Annick and Oliver Heal, and Anne-Marie and Gonzalg de Maupeou, who helped by welcoming my family and me into their homes and communities; their help made the difference between a difficult stay and an excellent sojourn. I would also like to give a special thanks to all the people in the Bigoudennie who took the time to explain the ways in which the fishing crisis intervened in their lives. To the men on the boats I sailed on (however briefly), met on the docks, at meetings, and in other less "formal" contexts, I wish you good fishing.

René-Pierre Chever, secretary general of the Comité local des pêches maritimes (CLPM), Pays Bigouden, went out of his way to introduce me to fishers and continues to support my efforts to better understand and to make known the world of fishing peoples. Several members of the CLPM executive made a special effort to assist my studies—André Le Berre (president of the CLPM 1995–2003; current president of the regional committee), Robert Boughéon (president of the CLPM 2003–present), Camille Gouzien (former vice-president), and Scarlette Le Corre (former vice-president). Pascal Boccou (Organisation des pêcheries de l'Ouest Bretagne) helped explain the crisis and the impact on Breton skippers near the beginning of my fieldwork. Franc Dorval (director, Cirée de St. Guénolé) was very helpful in describing the process of Saint Guénolé's fish auction and providing data on sales during my field period. Thank you also to Christine Nédélec (L'Association solidarité entreprises de pêche), Aimé Guegeun (Skipper), and Armand Le Cosec (Skipper).

Conversations and meetings with academics in Paris, Brest, Concarneau, Lorient, and Nantes were important for situating my work within the local context. My thanks especially to Alain Le Sann (Pêches et Dévelopement), Martine Segalen (Centre d'Ethnologie Française), Aliette Giestdoerfer (Université Paris-X), Patrick Dorval (UBO-Centre de Génie Industriel, Lorient), Patrick Chaumette (Université de Nantes), and Herve Gloux and Ahn Boclé-Gloux (formerly of the Musée de la Pêche, Concarneau). I have benefited greatly from the careful attention to detail of the UTP editorial and production staff that have made this final stage in the experience a real delight.

This project has been supported in part by a City University of New York pre-dissertation field trip grant, a Social Sciences and Humanities Research Council of Canada doctoral fellowship (1991–94), a doctoral research grant from the Wenner-Gren Foundation for Anthropological Research (1995–96), the Humanities and Social Science research fund at the University of British Columbia (1996–2002), the Social Sciences and Humanities Research Council of Canada standard research grant (2006–09), the Ethnographic Film Unit at UBC, and generous family support.

Thanks also to the tolerant management of two UBC coffee shops—The Original Beanery and Beans Around the World—where much of this book was written and rewritten. Writing is a solitary venture but best conducted, I believe, in the midst of the flux and noise of the world we live in.

Vancouver, BC

INTRODUCTION

But look! here come more crowds, pacing straight for the water, and seemingly bound for a dive. Strange! Nothing will content them but the extremest limit of the land; loitering under the shady lee of yonder warehouses will not suffice. No. They must get just as nigh the water as they possibly can without falling. And there they stand— miles of them—leagues. Inlanders all, they come from lanes and alleys, streets and avenues—north, east, south, and west.... Let the most absent-minded of men be plunged in his deepest reveries— stand that man on his legs, set his feet a-going, and he will infallibly lead you to water, if water there be in all that region.

—Herman Melville, *Moby-Dick; or the Whale* (1851)

SITUATING THE "FIELD"

I have been fascinated with the sea and the people who make their living from it from my childhood in coastal British Columbia through to my professional work as an anthropologist in Brittany. There is much to commend the Breton seascape: crisp blue skies in summer, angry grey banks of clouds in winter, and the veritable clichés of brightly coloured fishboats and the bustle of harbour life. All this can captivate and entertain casual visitor and seasoned traveller alike. There is an undeniable fascination that draws many of us, like Melville's narrator, to the edge of land where we gaze out expectantly

1

over the ocean. While I share Lévi-Strauss's concern to set my sojourn and observations apart from that of the "common tourist" or travel writer, there is much that connects the anthropological with the tourist gaze (1974). Yet if there is one aspect of our work as anthropologists that does set us apart and allow us the conceit of authority, it is the passage of time spent living within the communities that we write about.

Anthropologists have traditionally called the places or settings of our research the "field." We make a distinction between where and when we conduct our research and the place and time within which we write up our findings. In recent decades, this fairly simplistic distinction between field and home has become complicated by critique (Geertz 1988; see also Borneman and Hammoudi 2009) and advances in information technology. Nonetheless, practising anthropologists still refer to their place of research as the "field." As we go forward, we will learn about a place called Le Guilvinec and the Bigouden region of coastal France, the place that formed the field of my research.

The fishing port of Le Guilvinec is the economic centre of the Bigouden Region of Brittany. This book documents the historical and cultural context within which the local fishery emerged and developed. I bring to this discussion a deep-rooted empathy for fishing peoples. My hometown of Prince Rupert shares many superficial similarities with the Bigouden ports that I am writing about here. But it too has its own unique history. Whereas the intersection between agriculture and industrial development has been a key factor in the last hundred years of Bigouden history, in Prince Rupert local history has been shaped by the confluence of Aboriginal and settler lives.

Prince Rupert is located on the north Pacific coast of Canada. The people who live and work there come from all corners of the world. Elsewhere I have written about the history of Prince Rupert's fishery, its struggles, conflicts, and moments of happiness and accomplishment (Menzies 1990, 1992, 1993). As in the Bigouden region, our early commercial fisheries were part of a canning industry, but rather than sardines, my family fished for salmon, herring, and halibut. Canada's fisheries have also suffered crises. Ill-fated management plans have plunged fishing communities into decline. But, as in the **Bigoudennie**, fishers keep at it despite all of the difficulties and obstacles they face.

I also spent close to three decades working as a commercial fisherman. I first went to sea as a child on my family's fishboat; later, as an adult, I earned my living as a commercial fisherman. I no longer make my living by fishing—today I work in one of Canada's major research universities, the University of British Columbia. However, I have never truly left behind the sounds, smells, images, and memories that shaped who I am. During my sojourn in the Bigoudennie and the many trips back, I have often had the occasion to reflect upon my life as a son of a fisherman and upon my own time at sea. These memories and feelings form an underlying context through which my contemporary observations are filtered.

When I first visited coastal Brittany in the winter of 1992, I brought with me a list of potential field sites in which fishing was the primary economic activity. I was looking for an area with a small to medium-sized fishing fleet operated by family enterprises. Due to my theoretical interest in **social reproduction** and family enterprises, I immediately ruled out industrial ports such as Boulogne or Lorient. Instead, I concentrated on visiting the many small and out-of-the-way fishing villages that are spread along the Breton coast between St. Malo in the north and Vannes in the south.

As I toured the coast, many fishers were already talking about the developing crisis. They complained of poor fish prices, declining catches, and non–**European Union** (EU) fish imports. A major fishing co-operative had been forced to reorganize and consolidate its processing facilities due to economic exigency; in the process, nearly 100 workers lost their jobs. Fishing skippers were having difficulties paying their boat mortgages. The families of crewmembers had begun the process of economizing in the home.

Though the problems seemed to be widespread, it was in the **artisanal**[1] **fishing** ports of the Bigoudennie that they were most acute. This was so for two reasons. First, fishing forms the economic base of the region. In the industrial ports, while important, fishing is merely one among many economic engines. However, changes in fishing revenue in the Bigoudennie reverberated throughout the local economy and resulted in a generalized economic crisis. Second, and more importantly, the artisanal character of fishing in the Bigoudennie ensured that the crisis would be earlier and more intensely felt than in the industrial fisheries due to the importance of extended networks of kin and family in the fishery. Here the family networks of resource sharing revealed themselves. The decline in fishing income had a direct impact on the economic health of a wide network of people who were part of the many extended kindreds tied to fishing.

The men and women that I met during those years impressed me with their stories of current and past struggle. Even in the face of crisis, they saw the possibility of hope. They drew upon two symbols of their past in their current struggle—the **red flag** of international workers' struggle and the lace

---

[1] Artisanal here refers to a technical term used by the French to designate a specific class of fishing enterprises: boats under 24 metres in length, not owned by an incorporated firm.

coiffe of local tradition. I say more about these two symbols later (see Chapter Two). Here it is important to explain why I use them as the title of this book.

In the French context, the red flag is both an international symbol of working-class struggle and a local reference to the French Republic's own history of revolution and reaction. It is directly embedded within France's national tricolour flag of red (republic), white (the clergy and royalty), and blue (the bourgeoisie). Police reports of early-twentieth-century protests in the Bigoudennie describe the fishers rolling up the tricolour into an inflammatory red flag. Fishers told me about their family's and their region's history of labour struggle. They proudly recounted stories of their grandmothers who marched from the Port of Lesconil to Pont L'Abbé flying the red flag. At the same time, these grandmothers wore the traditional coiffe, a tall lace cylinder perched atop their heads. Flag and coiffe were described as being equally important: the red flag marked their determination, while the coiffe demonstrated commitment to their community. As we will see, there are many facets to these symbols and the stories they motivate. As it turns out, both flag and coiffe are of relatively recent origins. Nonetheless, they took on a special meaning in the context of the late-twentieth-century struggles for the survival of the Bigouden fisheries.

My impressions and observations from many years of research in the Bigoudennie are recorded in notebooks, files of documents and news clippings, and, more graphically, in the photos I took. Glancing through my family photo albums, I see the passage of more than two years in Brittany recorded from the perspective of everyday life. These photos mark the events, trips, birthdays, guests, anniversaries, and other moments of parenthood and family. The place—that is to say the field site—enters this record as glimpses of landscape and blurred backgrounds against which the normal life of the family progresses. Later photos, taken on return visits, tend to capture reunions with friends in their homes.

Thus, my experience of being in the Bigoudennie is overwritten by my experience as a father and as a partner to my wife. We attended the public school festival like the other parents. Some sunny afternoons we piled into our car and had a picnic on the beach, along some nearby lakeshore, or in a neighbouring wood. On my way home from the daily commercial fish auction, I often stopped to pick up a few things at the supermarket or bakery. These are not earth-shattering events but part of a life that continues irrespective of whether one is in France, Canada, the United States, or elsewhere.

One of our early arrivals in Brittany is captured in a series of pictures of my sons playing on a beach near our first temporary lodgings. It is late in the afternoon and the setting sun colours the landscape. In one picture, the boys are standing behind an inscription etched in the sand: "Jarek and Tristan,

FIGURE 0.1: Jarek and Tristan, 16 October 1994, Brittany

Oct. 16, 1994, Brittany." This photo masks the anxiety of navigating along highways and county lanes, searching out what is for us, strangers here, difficult and incomprehensible. Now, having finished with the necessities of shopping, signing leases, and cleaning up, we have retreated to this beach to relax and take stock of the place we shall call home for the next year or more.

In one of the few photos in which I am in the picture, I am standing on the edge of a quay in the Port of Lesconil. One boy is perched near the edge of the dock; I am holding the other on the seat of an adult's bike. Off to the side, an old-style **dragger** is coming alongside the dock. The white-washed sides of stone houses are just visible across the harbour. While my presence is clearly defined, the skipper of the dragger is barely a silhouette framed in the window of his wheelhouse. The clues to his identity are locked within the silhouette of the boat and in its registration number. Much can be learned from a reading of the boat: age, rigging, gear-type, crew size, port of registry, etc. However, these faceless and objective data push the skipper and his crew even further into the shadows.

My goal in this book is to bring the faces of these men and their families out of the shadows, to listen to their stories, to make sense of the silences and commemorations of local histories and past struggles. Ultimately, my aim is to locate the relevance of the remembered past in the moment of the current crisis, a crisis in which it seems that past lessons may no longer apply.

FIGURE 0.2: Author and sons on the dock at Lesconil

BEGINNING IN THE EARLY 1990s my research in the Bigouden region involved working with and talking to local fishers as they worked, and then later visiting them and their families at home. The daily rhythm of work in Le Guilvinec is set by the cycles of the seasons of fish and weather. For most of the year, the local fishboats depart early each weekday for the nearby fishing grounds. At the end of the day, each boat and its three- or four-man crew return to port to offload and sell their catch in the local fish auction. Waiting for them at day's end to help unload the boats are groups of men who are retired, unemployed, or on vacation. Watching from an observation deck overhead are dozens, at times hundreds, of tourists. Even in the middle of winter, a few onlookers are likely to be found waiting with camera at the ready to snap a memory of this picturesque scene.

Le Guilvinec and its three Bigouden sister ports (Penmarc'h-St. Guénolé, Lesconil[2] and Loctudy) comprise the leading artisanal fishing district in France and rank third overall in terms of landed value of fish. This small region on the edge of continental Europe has held tenaciously to its local

[2] Lesconil is more memory than reality as a fishing port today. It has suffered a serious decline in landings over the past decade or two, to the point of being economically non-viable.

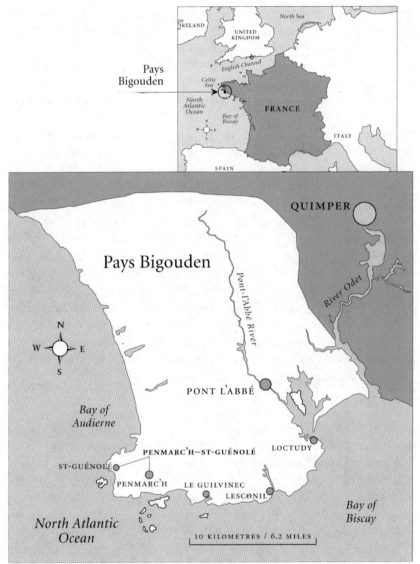

FIGURE 0.3: Map of Pays Bigouden

family-operated fishing fleet in the face of wave after wave of crisis. The turbulence of the fishery's real-time existence is obscured from the tourist gaze by the postcard-like scene of the fishing port. This is the backdrop against which and underneath which the ruptures and antagonisms of the daily politics to survive are played out.

Ethnographic experience—the actual lived experience of "being there"—lends anthropological writing its strength and allows particular insights into human society and culture. Anthropologists are observers of the everyday, the normal, the typical. This is the observational and interactive basis upon which anthropology rests and lays claim to its sense of authenticity (Borneman and Hammoudi 2009). But what of the situations in which the everyday is not normal, when the lessons of the past no longer help, when we must, as Gerald Sider asserts, act "against experience" (1997a; see also Sider 2003, 57)?

My account of the Bigouden fishery moves between the normalized world of the everyday and the intrusiveness of disruption and crisis that rocks small-scale fisheries globally. Analytically, it is the hidden, underlying socioeconomic processes that are propelling the disruptions in the lived experiences of the fisherfolk that this book is about. Yet, in their own worlds and experiences, whatever the ruptures, turbulences, and contradictions that "come to reshape everyday life" (Sider 2003, 58), these men and women experience it as ongoing and commonplace. Thus, my account is also about the ways in which people attempt to maintain their sense of continuity through the "ordinary routines of daily life, the mundane and comforting sameness of repetitive activities, such as drinking a cup of coffee with the morning newspaper. These activities give structure and logic to people's lives" (Becker 1997, 4). This is, ultimately, an awkward dance between explication of the underlying social and economic processes of the contemporary world and the subjective experiences and explanations of fishers in coastal Brittany.

IT IS MID-JULY 2009. The late-afternoon sun is glistening on the water. The approaching fishboats, decked out in bright colours, are returning to the harbour to unload. Gathered on the overhead observation deck, tourists point eagerly toward the incoming boats. The local men who help with the unloading are ready with handcarts piled with empty fish boxes. Under the unknowing gaze of the tourists, they persist in their struggle as artisanal fishers even as they become the backdrop to a tourist experience.

I have joined these men at the dock's edge today by squeezing through the narrow opening of the fence designed to keep the tourists out. The dockside arrangement has changed since the first time I stood here in 1994[3] waiting for the boats to come in. Then the dock was open to all, and the

---

[3] My field research in the Bigouden region began with an initial 12-week visit in 1992. In the fall of 1994, I returned with my family for an additional 14 months. I have returned to the Bigoudennie on an almost yearly basis since 1998. In 2006–07 I returned to produce a film about the tenacity of the local fishers and the ecological soundness of their approach to fishing (*Face à la tempête/Weather the Storm*, Bullfrog Films, 2008).

FIGURE 0.4: The fishboat *Odessa* docking in Le Guilvinec

throngs of summer tourists made life difficult for the men as they unloaded their boats and watched for their wives and children waiting to greet them. At that time, the fishery was in the midst of a major economic and ecological collapse. Fishing income had fallen by nearly 30 to 40 per cent, and the fish stocks were so overexploited as to be nearing commercial extinction. While the situation has improved over the intervening years, the crisis of the early 1990s left its mark. Since then, the number of boats and fishing jobs has fallen by more than a quarter. Incomes, while stabilized, are nowhere near the highs of the 1980s. While fishing remains the major force of the local economy, local development is now more explicitly oriented toward encouraging tourism.

I am looking forward to greeting my friend Jean-Jacques and the other men with whom he fishes on the *Odessa*. Despite all the odds, he and the others in this port have maintained their foothold as artisanal fishers. They stand as anachronisms in a global industry in which the concentration and rationalization of production is the norm. In their effort to survive, they have grabbed hold of a local history that gives meaning to their attachment to this place and good reason to continue to fight for a local family-based fishery.

WHERE IS THE BIGOUDENNIE?

Early in the fall of 1994, I was invited to attend a demonstration outside the courthouse in Nantes, 300 kilometres south of Le Guilvinec, in support of six men who had been charged with destroying fish during a demonstration the previous June. During the chartered bus trip there and back, as well as during the wait for the court case and decision, I had plenty of opportunity to talk about the problems in the fishery. In an important way, this trip broke the ice and allowed my research to move beyond the realm of officialdom to an engagement with the men I had only been observing as they unloaded their daily catch. It is to this group of men, their families, and friends that I most owe a debt of gratitude. While this work is the particular product of my vision and interpretation of my time in the Bigoudennie, it owes no small part to the company I kept on that rainy day in November.

The male world of the fishers is one bound in close personal ties, hard work, and often intense feelings of alienation from the wider society. This is a world that is often hard to enter. Non-fishers are by definition strangers, especially for the men working the boats. In the Bigoudennie, this is compounded by a tourist trade that, for certain weeks of the year, overwhelms the local population and plugs the roads, seashore, stores, and living space with voyeuristic outsiders. Other anthropologists have written of the necessity to move inland, away from the tourist press during the summer months, in order to avoid being confused with the tourists (cf. Badone 1989).

FIGURE 0.5: Police keeping fishers out of the court in Nantes

FIGURE 0.6: Author onboard commercial fishboat in British Columbia, circa 1985

My own life's work as a fisherman and a skipper's son both facilitated and made more difficult my time in the Bigoudennie. I actively made use of my understanding of fishing and work as a fisherman. I carried with me everywhere a small photo album of fishing boats, fish, and fishers from back home in Prince Rupert. Many long conversations and relationships emerged out of this small album. I was able to envision and empathize with the intimate experience and close-cutting ties that simultaneously unite and divide fishing communities. Yet my superficial familiarity was, to a certain extent, also a handicap. The world around me so closely reminded me of my own childhood and adult work experiences as to obscure at times what was uniquely Bigouden or European. Yet, for the Bigouden fishers I came to know, our common experience as fishers created the medium through which communication could proceed. That I was also a researcher affiliated with an American university further legitimated what was already understood as a valid professional interest in fisheries in general.[4]

I arrived in the Bigoudennie at the tail-end of the 1994 tourist season and with the first rains of winter. I was not alone in my interest in the local fishers. Television crews and radio and print journalists were gathered, waiting to see if for the third year in a row local fishers would again erupt into social protest. When nothing happened, the journalists turned to other issues. My arrival in the midst of a journalistic scrum helped to locate my interest as crucial. The fishers I knew interpreted my continuing presence in the Bigoudennie beyond the waning of journalistic interest as reflecting their own sense of the importance of the issue and my commitment toward understanding their crisis.

THE BIGOUDEN WORLD OF FISHERIES

Finistère comprises the western tip of Brittany; the southern part of it, the Bigoudennie, incorporates the cantons of Le Guilvinec, Pont L'Abbé, and Plogastel-St. Germain, an area of roughly 150 to 200 square kilometres characterized by intense cultural particularities (cf. Segalen 1991; Hélias 1978). The region is noted in travel guides and local histories for the unique lace coiffe worn by its women. The coiffe, a cylinder of lace fixed to the top of a small black bonnet, can be as high as 30 centimetres and was worn as an item of everyday clothing for a good part of the twentieth century. Today, only a few aged women continue to wear it on a daily basis, while younger

---

[4] During my initial fieldwork I was a graduate student at the City University of New York. Subsequent field research was conducted while a faculty member at the University of British Columbia.

women wear it occasionally for special holidays, folk festivals, and pan-Celtic celebrations. In the context of the political struggles of the 1990s, the coiffe was deployed in an assembly of symbols denoting a sense of belonging and Bigouden identity.

The Bigouden coastline consists of open sandy beaches occasionally broken by rocky outcroppings. The region is effectively demarcated on the west and south by ocean and on the east by the river Odet. The northerly frontier winds along a low-lying stream valley, which opens at the sea town of Audierne. The land is not particularly suited to large-scale agriculture nor the intensive farming techniques adopted in the northern part of Finistère during the rapid **modernization** of the 1960s and 1970s. Prior to the commercial sardine fishery of the late 1880s, generations of **peasants** eked out a livelihood living near the coastal strip, alternating between land and sea.

The Bigoudennie is encapsulated in the maritime administrative district of Le Guilvinec, which incorporates the four fish ports of Le Guilvinec, Penmarc'h-St. Guénolé, Lesconil, and Loctudy, plus a number of small coves. Le Guilvinec, located in the centre of the southern coast, lends its name to the district. To the west, Penmarc'h-St. Guénolé juts out into the Atlantic. To the east is Lesconil. Finally, Loctudy is located at the mouth of the river of Pont L'Abbé. Each of these ports carries a unique local history of development that reflects the intersection of contemporary forces and historical antecedents.

Penmarc'h-St. Guénolé is the elder sister of the Bigouden ports. During the fifteenth and sixteenth centuries, it was a significant merchant port with nearly 300 coastal traders registered. The local boats plied the lucrative trading routes ranging south to Bordeaux and as far north as the Low Countries and the British Isles. The nearby cod banks (now essentially extinct) were regularly visited by the European salt-cod fleets until the discovery of the rich fishing grounds off Newfoundland. By the end of the seventeenth century, Penmarc'h-St. Guénolé's fortunes were on the decline. It wouldn't be until the late nineteenth century that the economic well-being of the port approached its earlier level with the development of the industrial sardine fishery.

Lesconil today is a mere shell of its former self. With only eight boats left that regularly sell to its daily auction,[5] it is well on the way to being a tourist

---

[5] Each of the four Bigouden fish ports has (or in Lesconil's case, had) a government-managed fresh-fish auction where the fishers are able to sell their daily catch to fish processors and fishmongers who in turn prepare the fish for sale in the regional, national, and international fish markets.

port with a fishing ambience. Once a key location of militant **strikes** during the sardine crisis of the early twentieth century, today it is rapidly being engulfed by the expanding tourist trade and housing redevelopment that is underway in the coastal zones of Brittany.

Loctudy was a merchant shipping and fishing port for several centuries. In its earliest formations, it was known for its lumber and grain exports. A growing regional potato crop became an important export in the early nineteenth century, especially during the Irish Famine of the early 1800s when the village became almost completely focused on the export of potatoes. With the rapid expansion of the canned sardine fishery of the late 1800s, Loctudy regained its focus on fisheries and today boasts an active fleet of **trawlers** that make two-week trips to fish in the Irish Sea, a modest fleet of smaller boats that deliver to the daily fish auction, and a growing recreational boating sector.

Le Guilvinec is the undisputed first port of the four and for over 100 years has been the dynamic centre of the local fishing industry. From 24-metre vessels fishing the Irish Sea to smaller coastal trawlers (10–20 metres) and even smaller **trap, longline,** and **gillnet** boats (2–10 metres), the port supports a bustling variety of activities. While tourism is pressing hard on the city, no visitor will mistake this port for anything other than what it is—a commercial fish port.

Pont L'Abbé is the commercial centre of the Bigouden Region, shipping timber, grains, and potatoes through most of its history. However, with the development of commercial fisheries in the late 1800s and the rise of rail transport, Pont L'Abbé rapidly lost its importance as a commercial port. By the early 1930s, commercial activities were essentially over. Today the vestiges of old warehouses and quays can be seen along the entrance to the town, and a scattering of pleasure craft are anchored there.

ASPECTS OF THE LOCAL ECONOMY

The fishery, with its associated support industries, is the motor of the local economy. Service-sector employment is secondary and relies on the existence of a strong fishery for its survival. The majority of industrial jobs are in such support industries as fish processing, boat building and repair, and other ancillary sectors. It is unlikely that any of these industrial jobs would exist at all without the fishery.

There is an important link between the fishery and the region's overall economic health. The development of the welfare state in the form of public-sector employment in this region has acted to modify cyclical swings and dampen the extent of crises. It has not, however, replaced the crucial importance of the productive sectors of the economy. Furthermore, throughout the late 1980s and 1990s, welfare-state support had been progressively eroded. Hence the increasing local reliance upon the fishery as the primary source of economic sustenance, even during periods of crisis in the fishery.

Agriculture, once predominant in this region, has been in decline since the 1960s. Between 1970 and 1980, almost one-third of the farms in the Bigoudennie disappeared, while the average age of those working them rose (Segalen 1991, 250). By the late 1990s, the number of active farms had plummeted from 1,094 in 1970 to just 135. The decrease in units of exploitation and the area under cultivation has been matched by an increase in the average size of individual farms from nine hectares in 1970 to 24 in 1991 (Cleac'h and Piriou 1993). The decline of agriculture in the region is inscribed on the landscape by an increase in fallow lands and abandoned farmhouses as the cost of remaining on the land has outstripped the cost of abandonment or letting it sit fallow. Farmhouses have been turned into holiday homes, and the nature of the once agricultural landscape has been irrevocably changed.

The local tourist industry is based on a short seaside summer season that provides immediate returns for a few but does very little in terms of providing for long-term economic stability. Most of the summer tourist trade consists of cottagers and campers who come from Paris and Germany or across the channel from Britain to holiday on local beaches such as the renowned surfing beach at La Torche.

According to Le Bail and Nicot (1995), it is unlikely that tourism will replace fishing in the foreseeable future as a significant source of alternative employment. Squeezed as it is into July and August, the seaside tourist industry is able to create only a short-term demand for summer employment in the cafes, restaurants, hotels, and campgrounds. Firms with more than ten employees (8 per cent of their winter workforce) add an additional 440 individuals during the tourist season. Smaller firms (cafes, hotels, and restaurants, etc.) increase their workforce by 72 per cent or 322 individuals.

The interface between tourism and the fishery is most obvious during the unloading of boats in July and August. Until the late 1990s, the dock was jammed with tourists from France, Germany, and Britain who jostled one another to see the fish being passed off the boats by hand, box by box. The fishers found themselves forced to move their heavily laden fish carts through a press of tourists unwilling to give way until the last possible moment. By the end of July, many of the men had stopped yelling out a warning as they hurtled pell-mell through the mass of tourists.

The situation at the unloading dock eventually became untenable, and the fishers pressured the port authority to keep the dock clear during the

FIGURE 0.7: Unloading fishboat, with tourists looking on from overhead deck

tourist season. Now tourists who arrive in July or August are directed to a viewing area overlooking the unloading dock. To capitalize on the opportunity, the town and the port authority opened a fishing museum and display in 2000 that tourists can visit while waiting for the fishing fleet to return to port. From its deck, the tourists can look down over the fish auction floor or even sign up for a tour of the auction itself or for a day at sea on a local fishboat.

HISTORICAL CONTEXT

The commercial fishery in this region has its roots in the recent past. After an interregnum of more than two centuries (there had once been a thriving salt-cod fishery in the region), a commercial sardine fishery emerged in the late 1800s. The canning industry in coastal Bigoudennie was spearheaded by industrial firms who, for the most part, were already operating canning plants in Nantes, Concarneau, or Brest (Boulard 1991; Guégruen and Le Maitre 1990). The first plant in Le Guilvinec opened in 1864. However, it wasn't until the railway was extended to Pont L'Abbé in 1884 that the industrialization of coastal Bigoudennie took off. The growth of the fishery marked the turn from an agrarian-peasant economy to an industrial-capitalist economy.

In the Bigoudennie, the change from an agricultural to industrial fishing economy occurred quickly and dramatically. For example, between the years 1880 and 1890 the hamlet of Le Guilvinec grew from fewer than 100 residents to a small town of more than 6,000. The living conditions were atrocious, as the profits gained by the cannery owners were not passed on to their workers. The spacious homes of the owners and managers stood in stark contrast to the squalid and cramped homes that housed the newly formed working class. Between 1890 and 1910, three separate cholera epidemics swept through the fishing towns. Tuberculosis was rampant, life expectancy dropped, and infant mortality increased. Not until well into the 1920s did basic health and sanitary conditions return to the level at which they had been when agriculture was the primary economic activity.[6]

The social transformation from peasant to fishworker was accompanied by militant trade unionism. From **Luddite** struggles against the introduction of the labour-saving "*sertiers*" (which replaced the hand soldering of sardine cans with a highly efficient mechanical process and thereby eliminated several hundred relatively well-paid fishworkers) to strikes over the minimum prices for fish, coastal Bigoudennie was a cauldron of social unrest.

During the **Sardine Years** (1864–1936), the canneries controlled many aspects of their workers' lives. They availed themselves of every resource of intimidation to prevent disruption of the smooth functioning of business. In a letter dated 1905, one cannery manager complained to the **prefect** in Quimper that a wave of revolution was sweeping across the department and

---

[6] Archives départementales (hereafter identified as AD), Quimper: File 4S 356–61.

must be at all costs put down. The prefect responded by sending a unit of mounted police to ensure that the local cannery could operate without interruption. In the face of the collusion between state and business, skippers, crews, and cannery workers organized themselves into unions.[7]

At the national political level, the industry has been buffeted throughout its history by alternating periods of economic liberalism and protectionism. The development of the early sardine fishery greatly benefited from a strongly protectionist economic policy, which made it difficult for sardines from Spain and Portugal to enter the French market. However, the simultaneous internationalization of capital allowed the canning firms to relocate and leave behind starving fishers and fishworkers. For example, most of the canneries operating in coastal Bigouden also operated plants in Portugal, Spain, or North Africa. Therefore, they were interested in maintaining liberal trade policies and introducing more efficient canning techniques in their French plants.

The evolution of **fishing gear** and vessels also progressed rapidly during the twentieth century. The first diesel-powered fishing vessels (14- to 20-metre wooden draggers) began replacing the earlier sailing vessels by the 1930s. The change in propulsion systems opened the way for the development and expansion of major artisanal fishing ports such as Le Guilvinec. Fishers were able to move farther afield under increasingly inclement conditions, and the variety of fish available to be caught correspondingly increased.

In the years following the Second World War, the **catching capacity** of the French fishing fleet expanded at an astronomical rate. Fuelled by government funding and the need for food products in war-ravaged Europe, the industry expanded with little consideration for the ecological health of the fisheries resource. On the technological end, overcapacity was generated by the rapid introduction of new types of fishing gear, more powerful engines, hydraulics, electricity, navigational and communications equipment, and new stronger types of building materials (steel, aluminum, and fibreglass) for boats and machinery.

Nonetheless, the development of the French welfare state coincided with the decline of the industrial sardine canning industry. While it is prudent to caution against drawing too hasty a conclusion, neither should one under-

---

[7] AD, Quimper: File 4S 358. Fishers—skippers and crews—organized jointly and in opposition to the industrial canners. This form of union organization continues to be the model followed in the region. However, during the early 1990s the left-oriented union Force Ouvrière (FO) began organizing the crewmembers on the 24-metre class draggers fishing out of Loctudy. FO organizers accused the national labour unions, the CGT and CFDT, of being ineffective representatives of the crews.

estimate the role of state intervention in this change. For example, in correspondence between cannery owners and state officials during the period 1903–14, the canners advocated state intervention in the fishery, and state officials complied without apparent protest. It is important to point out that the state's response was not simply one of armed intervention but—and this is a crucial point—also in funding credit unions to assist fishers in buying and modernizing their fishing boats and gear. One unintended by-product of the state-funded credit union was that it generated the economic means for local fishers to escape the direct control of the industrial canners. Paradoxically, the timely intervention of the state contributed to the withdrawal of the industrial canning industry from the region.

The postwar French state was shaped by **Charles de Gaulle**'s conservative **corporatism**. In the face of a strong communist and socialist opposition, he introduced a variety of social welfare measures in an attempt to prevent a communist takeover of the state apparatus. De Gaulle also instituted enterprise and industry-wide committees, which included representatives from all segments of each industry; for example, the local, regional, and national fishing committees represent deckhands, skippers, industrial fishing companies, processors, and distributors.

The underlying assumption of the corporatist model was that these committees would engender a spirit of tripartite co-operation between government, labour, and business that would forestall more radical action on the part of subaltern groups. However, the increasing degree of state intervention merely served to define the site and target of political protest as lying within the realm of the state, not of capital. The corporatist Gaullist state strove to incorporate working-class demands within the context of a capitalist state without threatening the stability of business. The essence of the tactic "is that in return for consultation and a representational monopoly within their sphere, each co-party exerts control over the base of their organization" (Gough 1979, 146). This is physically manifest in the Bigoudennie through the local fishing committee, the **Comité local des pêches maritimes** (CLPM). However, the existence of such bodies does not preclude social conflict. When conflict does break out, as it did in 1994–95, it tends to be more aligned in opposition to state policies than as a more "straightforward" worker/employer struggle.

BIGOUDEN ISOLATION AND INTEGRATION

The wave of industrialization that swept along the Breton coastline in the latter third of the nineteenth century had a major impact on the shape of the region known today as the Bigoudennie—not in the sense of the "modernization" of an isolated rural region but rather in laying down the foundations upon which contemporary economic processes of integration and isolation are now being acted.

The issue of "isolation" is important because the dominant discourse in popular and academic discussion of Brittany (see, for example, Badone 1989; Weber 1976; Morin 1967) focuses upon the false dichotomy between rural isolation/traditionalism and modernization/integration. The very issue of isolation versus integration obscures important underlying processes and linkages. Within these processes, isolation and integration are simply conjoined aspects of a single system of trade and production in which physical connections to the outside have emerged and then retreated over the course of several centuries.

For Eugen Weber (1976), the years between 1870 and 1914 (*la belle époque*) ushered in a period of change and integration that ultimately led to the transformation of "peasants into Frenchmen." Weber points to the rapid expansion of the instruments of civil society, most notably education and communications, as being pivotal in this process. According to him, the years of *la belle époque* were witnesses to a multitude of "distinct societies" (to borrow from the Canada/Québec dialogue) being dissolved into a homogenous "French" identity. While the implications of standardized education, rail transportation, industrialization, and the commercialization of agriculture undoubtedly changed the social and political "face" of France, it is debatable whether the process of conformity and homogenization that Weber suggests in fact occurred (see, for example, Lehning 1995; Magraw 1983).

Generally speaking, Weber stresses the rather benign impact of incorporation into a national state and invokes a mythic rural France shuttered behind the cloisters of superstition and ignorance. Yet, as Magraw suggests:

> it could be argued [contra Weber] that the nineteenth-century developments made the countryside more rural and "peasantized," less "modern" if one wishes to use that terminology. For not only did rural outworkers succumb to factory competition, but many of those literate, radical culture-brokers who had provided the contacts between the peasantry and the urban world in 1848–51—wood floaters on the Yonne, carters, barges, blacksmiths, village shoemakers, Provençal cork and barrel-makers—were precisely the groups hit by urban competition, or by changes in transport, who quit the villages first, along with agricultural labourers, who declined from 4.5 to 3 million between 1860 and the 1900s. (1983, 321)

The point is that isolation and integration run hand in hand. As discussed later in this book, the development of a local Bigouden identity is as much a product of the period of industrialization in the fishery as it is of the region's isolation in physical terms from metropolitan France.

While the Bigoudennie may have been isolated from the administrative centre of France, it has not always been outside the orbits of major communication links and transportation routes. For example, local historian Serge Duigou documents the fact that the Bigoudennie boasted a fleet of some 270 vessels engaged in the Bordeaux–England wine trade in the fifteenth and sixteenth centuries (1991, 3–6; 1994). During this period, Penmarc'h-St. Guénolé was a bustling seaport of 11,000 inhabitants. Its mariners combined fishing with coastal trading and held a partial monopoly over the trade of wine. Their primary contracts were with the merchants of Bordeaux and Toulouse. Several worked for the British, the Spanish, and the Dutch as well. They were also involved in the fish trade, bringing their catches of dried cod to major ports in France, Spain, and Portugal. This period was marked by the affluence of the marine trade, the vestiges of which can still be seen in such places as the ruins of a large church tower standing in the centre of the village.

In the nineteenth century, fewer people lived in coastal Bigoudennie than had lived in the port of Penmarc'h-St. Guénolé alone during the fifteenth and sixteenth centuries. Situated within the context of potential surplus labour in the rural economy, the extension of rail transport, and a protected national market for sardines, the population of coastal Bigoudennie almost doubled between 1881 and the First World War. For the coastal communes of Treffiagat, Penmarc'h-St. Guénolé, Le Guilvinec, Pont L'Abbé, and Plomeur, the combined populations rose from 11,698 in 1881 to 22,022 in 1911. This coastal demographic explosion was a direct response to the spread of the canning industry into the area. Rural inland Bigouden communes show a much smaller increase or a stabilization of population at the 1881 levels and then a decline following 1911; for example, St. Jean-Trolimon rose from 986 in 1881 to only 1,124 in 1911. The decline in coastal populations occurred close to 50 years after that of interior communes such as St. Jean-Trolimon.

All this is to point out that the notion of an "isolated" peasantry waiting for the railway to wake it from its slumber and join the "modern" world is problematic at best, myopic at worst. The relationship between the local and the larger is not simply decipherable in terms of, for example, length of rail track or number of machines. This form of "muscular materialism"—obsessively focused on technological innovation and detailed counting of objects— deflects our quest to understand the messiness of everyday life. Undeniably, such counting, measuring, and detailing of objects is important. However, it is the social relations incorporating production and reproduction that ultimately drive the development and implementation of technology.

The process of change in the Bigoudennie is not isolated from global forces. Local agency, for example, is mediated or limited by the specificities of the wider socio-economic environment within which the local is encapsulated. During the global boom years in the Euro-American economy following the Second World War, working people were able to extend their notions of collective social benefits.[8] By the 1970s, however, working-class struggles became increasingly defensive. The provisions of the welfare state were less able to ameliorate the ill effects of **capitalism** and, in fact, became a shackle on the process of accumulation. Capital sought changes to regimes of production, social safety nets, and national controls over the movement of capital and goods (Ahmad 1992; Callinicos 1989; Palmer 1990). Three key features of late-twentieth-century capitalism are thus important to take note of: (1) changes in the organization of production from large, centrally located factories to an array of smaller, "flexible" units of sub-contractors; (2) the privatization of state firms and services, and the dismantling of the social safety net; and, (3) the globalization of the economy in such a way that the ability of the national state to independently regulate its own economy is no longer assured.

In the late twentieth century, the process of production underwent a re-spatialization. Work, originally located in factories employing several hundred people or more, was shifted out to small jobbers who in turn sub-contracted the work out in a manner reminiscent of the industrial out-workers described by E.P. Thompson in nineteenth-century England (1963, 288–89, 297–346). In this transition, capital effectively dispersed both economic risk and productive activities through outsourcing the production process.

A variety of labels have been presented to describe the current period, including, but not limited to, post-industrial, post-Fordist, and post-modern. These labels are united in their assertion that our current period is post-*something*. Often seen as an inevitable product of "neutral" technological advances, post-*somethingism* does accurately capture an essential respatialization of the process of production and a move toward more flexible units of production in which the economic risks are shifted outward and away from the central corporation (Harvey 1989). However, this approach tends to overemphasize the newness of the current moment and the extent to which fundamental change has occurred (Wood 1996).

---

[8] Across the Euro-American world, working-class movements secured benefits that went beyond workplace issues and extended into the structures of the Keynesian welfare state. The postwar situation of Canadian workers described by Bryan Palmer was generally reflective of most workers within the Euro-American world: "For the first time ever organized labour managed to force some semblance of security from capital and state, with the result that many of its ranks could actually settle into lives where stability was not undercut at every turn" (1992, 336).

A similar development has occurred throughout many of the world's commercial fisheries. Large processing firms have sold off their fleets of fishboats to ostensibly independent fishers. The boat owners operate under the illusion of freedom but are, in reality, still firmly under the control of large capital. Artisanal boat owners become, in essence, workers who must buy their own tools in order to work. Their class location is, however, complicated by their ownership of productive property. And, with respect to their crews, they take on the appearance of capital (see, for example, Clement 1986; Sinclair 1985). As Benton points out, in a case study of the Spanish shoe industry, "decentralization soon showed itself to have unexpectedly positive implications—from the point of view of employers—for the problem of control within the factories. Within formal firms, workers find their position so weakened [due to the existence of the new informal firms] that they must heed employers' demands to intensify work and increase the number of hours worked" (1990, 160).

Despite the respatialization of production, the fundamental aspect of the relationship between worker and employer has not altered. Theorists who argue that the socio-economic changes of the late twentieth century are of an epochal nature have "explicitly or implicitly, based their arguments on a theory of history that downplays the discontinuities *between* capitalist and non-capitalist societies, a theory that disguises the historical specificity of capitalism" (Wood 1996, 25). Fordist forms of production were first introduced to de-skill artisanal workers and to take control of production out of their hands and place it firmly within the orbit of capital. The collectivization of work, however, contributed to worker militancy. The process of decentralization of production—post-Fordism—today is best understood within this context.

Between the sardine crisis in the early 1900s and the more recent crisis in the 1990s, the Bigouden regional economy was completely transformed. The combination of changes in patterns of consumption, technologies, and the global capitalist system undermined the basis for industrial production in the region and left an **artisanal fishery** in its wake. Yet the fishery and its shore-based support industries are still the most important aspects of the local economy.

The contemporary Bigouden fishery operates within a socio-economic matrix that simultaneously includes new forms of information technologies to assist in the delivery of fresh fish to market as needed and at optimal prices; old forms of capital/labour relations (represented onboard the boats by skippers and crews); and kin-ordered systems of resource pooling, labour recruitment, and processes of economizing.

PART ONE

A LOCAL POLITICS
OF SURVIVAL

He looked across the sea and knew how alone he was now. But he could see the prisms in the deep dark water and the line stretching ahead and the strange undulation of the calm. The clouds were building up now for the trade wind and he looked ahead and saw a flight of wild ducks etching themselves against the sky over water, then blurring, then etching again and he knew no man was ever alone on the sea.

—Ernest Hemingway, *The Old Man and the Sea* (1952)

STORIES ABOUT FISHERS are very often tales of individualism, of one man against the elements. They speak to our society's interest and concern with the individual and the vicissitudes of fate and circumstance. Hemingway's old man takes on what may be the struggle of his individual life. His luck has run dry. He goes far out into the deep ocean in a small open skiff in pursuit of a big fish. Yet even in the midst of his solitary pursuit, the old man reminds us that "no man was ever alone on the sea."

This is an important point. While good fiction may need strong central characters, real-life changes emerge from the collective action of many individuals. In the following chapters, I explore three specific periods of struggle and their implications for a local conception of the politics of identity as it is linked to the ideas of struggle and survival in the contemporary Bigoudennie. I begin with the stories of the wave of strikes of the mid-1990s and the more restrained but equally important attempts to expand local resistance onto the global stage, and then I move the story backwards through historical time. While a different account might well start in the past and move forward, I have chosen to follow the narrative progression of the participants in the contemporary social movement because the meaning—the strategic importance—of this history lies in the manner in which it intersects, shapes, and haunts the struggles of the present.

SOCIAL STRUGGLE AT "LA FIN DE SIÈCLE"

THE MEN AND WOMEN I MET IN THE BIGOUDENNIE spoke of the burden imposed upon them by bureaucrats in Paris and Brussels. The bureaucrats stood as outsiders, unfamiliar and self-serving, to the local sense of community that connected artisanal fishers, irrespective of whether or not they owned boats, to their crews and the women and men who laboured ashore in the various support industries in the province. While the bureaucrats cut away fiscal supports, imposed ever more stringent regulations on their fishing efforts, and opened the doors of Europe ever wider to the flows of international trade, people in the Bigoudennie located this moment of crisis within a history of resistance and struggle in which outsiders were a constant threat to the survival of their community.

NIGHT OF FIRE

On the night of 22 February 1993, 800 to 1,000 Breton boat owners, crew-members, and their supporters stormed the wholesale fish auction in Rungis, just south of Paris. In the ensuing mêlée, 800 tons of fish valued at more than $4 million were destroyed. The fishers and their supporters engaged in a running battle with the **Force of Order** (as the specially trained French paramilitary riot police are called). Armed only with sticks and the brute determination of a people fighting for their livelihood, they held off the police until well into the early hours of the morning.

Many of the demonstrators came from the Breton fishing ports of Le Guilvinec, Douarnenez, and Concarneau, where earlier in the day more than 9,000 people had participated in demonstrations against changes in the

Common Fisheries Policy (CFP) of the European Union (EU). The new policies cut quotas, forced a reduction in the size of the French fishing fleet, and liberalized regulations governing the importation of non-EU fish products. The anger and strength of this and subsequent demonstrations underlined the extent of the crisis that shook the French artisanal fisheries in the early 1990s.

The fishers' protest movement was steeped in a language of the local and invoked symbols of the region's agrarian past. It eschewed a discourse of class, apparently as a mobilization tactic, emphasizing instead a strong sense of local solidarity and community. In the context of the reorganization of production in late capitalism, the terrain of production, and hence struggle, has shifted. The state has, to a large extent, replaced capitalist firms as the primary pole of struggle *vis-à-vis* boat owners and hired crews.

This is so in two senses. First, the state plays a fundamental role in the regulation of the fisheries. This is compounded in France by the provisions of the EU Common Fisheries Policy, which governs all fishing outside of a narrow 12-mile coastal strip. In other words, there are two specific levels of governance regulating the process of production on the fishboat and within the local community. Second, the state (again at both the national and EU levels) finances and, through a variety of provisions, controls crucial economic structures such as boat loans, marketing and processing facilities, and minimum prices for key fish species.

The CFP emerged out of the recognition that a Europe-wide regulatory framework was required. The first CFP, adopted 20 October 1970, set out two fundamental points: (1) equal access to the basic resource by all member states, and (2) a common market organization for fish similar to the common market for key agricultural products (Leigh 1983). This agreement still left much of the actual control of fisheries in the hands of individual member states and emphasized economic development, fleet modernization, and rationalization ahead of issues of conservation. The EU was not able to come to an agreement on a CFP that effectively dealt with both economic and conservation factors until January 1983 (Farnell and Elles 1984; Leigh 1983; Wise 1984; Holden 1994) when it gave the European Commission powers to set fishing quotas for member states, to limit access to fishing grounds, and to restrict fishing effort.

Fisheries policies have typically focused on regulating the harvesting side of the fishery. This sets off a struggle between regulators and fishers with each trying to outguess and outmanoeuvre the other in the struggle over the harvesting of fish. Caroline Butler (2005), writing about the fishers' response to impending regulatory changes, describes this as "fear fishing": a situation in which fishers ramp up their fishing effort in advance of impend-

FIGURE 1.1: Thousands demonstrate in support of the fishing industry, Le Guilvinec

ing regulatory changes. If left to self-regulate, artisanal fishers tend toward sustainable practices. However, the driving force of global markets and bio-economic fisheries management often compels local fishers to act against their own best interests and increase their fishing effort. Regulators have typically responded by: (1) creating vessel limitations in terms of size, power, or capacity; (2) decommissioning vessels; (3) restricting fishing effort through regulating fishing gear or limiting the number of days at sea; or (4) introducing individual transferable or vessel quotas (ITQs or IVQs).

1. *Vessel limitations.* The underlying approach here is that both the size, power, or carrying capacity of a fishing vessel and the number of fishing vessels in a fleet have a direct relationship to the amount of fish that will be caught. While such limitations do indeed have an impact on the catching capacity of individual vessels, vessel limitations have been fraught with a myriad of problems as fishers seek creative ways to circumvent regulations without actually breaking them. A particularly vexing problem of limitations on vessels is that they often have the paradoxical result of expanding, not restricting, catching capacity.

   Limitations on kilowatts of power in the French fleet have contributed to a refurbishment of the dragger. In this case, newer vessels far more efficient than their predecessors replace older, less efficient vessels. In British Columbia, a "limited entry" plan, which "froze" the fishing fleet at its 1968 level, resulted in the expansion of one sector of the fleet (the larger, more effective **seine** fleet) at the expense of the smaller, community-based gill-netters and trollers. Under the initial plan, fishers were able to combine licences from smaller boats in order to build larger, more efficient ones. As the process continued, fishers found that with the aid of naval architects, they could build bigger and better boats with smaller and smaller licences. When the government regulator finally introduced a length restriction and barred combining tonnage, it was too late.

   The difficulty with limited entry programs or limitations on vessel dimensions and power is that the underlying problems of competition and expanding fishing effort are not adequately addressed. In open access fisheries, fishing effort expands through increasing the number of fishboats. However, with limited entry, expanding fishing effort leads toward increases in capital invested in the boat. Thus, fishers invest more money in improving the capability of their vessel so that they can fish farther afield and in rougher weather. Government aid programs designed to assist fishers in modernizing their boats intercede in a contradictory manner and, ultimately, undermine attempts to control fishing effort.

FIGURE 1.2: Decommissioning the fishboat *Anthony Virginie*, Le Guilvinec Port

2. *Decommissioning or "buying back" vessels.* A variety of different types of decommissioning or "buy-back" schemes have been introduced across the world's fisheries. In France, vessels have been removed from the fishery by paying boat owners to destroy them. Boat owners have been very successful in reinvesting the government buyout in newer, more efficient vessels. Resource managers have simplistically assumed that the removal of any one unit of production (i.e., any one boat) will lead directly to a proportionate reduction in fishing effort. This has not been the case. In just about every documented example of fleet reductions through buy-backs or decommissioning, the actual catch of the remaining fleet has not declined. Nor has the "capacity" of the fleet decreased.

3. *Restricting fishing effort.* Placing restrictions on fishing effort by focusing on the type of gear or days at sea (in some cases "minutes" at sea is more accurate) has been the primary means of regulating fisheries. Fishers face regulations concerning mesh size, net length and depth, and the specific type of gear allowed (i.e., pots, **trawls**, hook and line, seines, traps, etc.). The dominant measure, fishing effort, is calculated in quantity of fish per unit of gear. Clearly, management plans designed to restrict fishing effort are by definition also plans to create inefficiency, which runs counter to the fishers' goal of improved efficiency; hence the fundamental line of conflict between fishers and resource managers. One of the primary methods to overcome the dialectic of efficiency/inefficiency inherent in all

previous management practices is the introduction of a variety of quota systems held by the individual boat owner.

4. *Individual transferable or vessel quotas (ITQs or IVQs).* Introduced in New Zealand, the United States, and Canada in the 1980s, this approach to resource management has gained rapidly in appeal among resource managers. The primary feature of the Individual Vessel Quota system (IVQ) is the privatization of the fishery in the hands of fishers or fishing enterprises. In theory, the IVQ motivates fishers to maximize their revenues and minimize their costs to earn the highest possible profit on their quota. In practice, this means deckhands lose jobs and licences are concentrated in corporate hands. The primary appeal of the IVQ for resource managers and fisheries economists is the relatively low cost of management and the system's theoretical emphasis on private property rights.

In combination, these fisheries management approaches have led to an expanded role for the state in regulating the harvesting of fish. This expansion has occurred within a context of what appears to be a fundamental shift in the capitalist organization of production. That change has occurred is uncontroversial and has been documented by many observers (Bluestone and Harrison 1982; Harvey 1989; Smith 1991; Blim 1992). In fact, the constant changes of production, built environment, and social arrangements is one of, if not the, fundamental aspects of capitalism in which "All fixed, fast-frozen relations, with their train of ancient and venerable prejudices and opinions, are swept away, all new-formed ones become antiquated before they can ossify. All that is solid melts into air, all that is holy is profaned, and man is at last compelled to face with sober senses, his real conditions of life, and his relations with his kind" (Marx and Engels 1969, 111). What is controversial is the nature of the current changes, which represent a radical disjuncture from early twentieth-century capitalism and what is considered the defining Fordist form of production. For some scholars employing post-modernist theories, in "contemporary high tech media society, emergent processes of change and transformation are producing a post-modern society ... the era of post-modernity constitutes a novel stage of history and novel socio-cultural formation" (Best and Kellner 1991, 3; see also, Luke 1989). Changes in the organization of production, while important, receive relatively little attention in this broader, more cultural formulation.

Moreover, according to Laclau and Mouffe (1985), capital has been so thoroughly reorganized that the working class is no longer the "gravedigger" of capitalism but rather one of its staunchest allies. New forms of class cleavage have been identified:

A line of conflict forms between, on the one hand, a center composed of strata directly involved in the production process and interested in maintaining capitalist growth on the basis of the welfare-state compromise, and, on the other hand, a periphery composed of a variegated array of groups that are lumped together. Among the latter are those groups that are further removed from the "productivist core of performance" in late capitalist societies, that have been more strongly sensitized to the self-destructive consequences of growth in complexity or have been more strongly affected by them. (Habermas 1986, 392–93)

Habermas is referring here to the so-called *new social movements* (NSM)—environmentalism, peace and nuclear disarmament activists, gay and lesbian activists—which sprang up in the aftermath of the New Left of the late 1960s. According to Timothy Luke, NSM are seen to "express organizationally a series of new territorial culture, functional cleavages, new classes" (Luke 1989, 137). The environmental movement, for example, is considered to represent a new class struggle against "unequal exchange and ecological colonialization by the core regions" (145). The most telling change in the *post-industrial* world for scholars such as Luke has been the rise of information technologies and the deindustrialization of Western economies. Accordingly, the NSM are seen as part of a "critical historical shift of a 'third industrial revolution'" (133).

The fishers' community-based protest movement confronts the myth of NSM theory. By exploring how a coalition of boat owners was able to mobilize support from their crews through a careful manipulation of symbols of class struggle and local identity, we can learn how **social class** is still the underlying structure of so-called identity politics. The crucial point here is that the class interests of a group of petty capitalists struggling to maintain their socioeconomic location within a rapidly shifting and changing field trumped identity politics. That their movement took on the contrived aura of local identity reflects the particularities of local history. That it was grounded in the political and economic power of the boat owners reveals contemporary economic reality.

ON TO CRISIS

The malaise faced by Breton fisherfolk grew sporadically after the end of the Second World War. There were three interrelated processes at work: technological developments, stock depletion, and government attempts at regulation. Under postwar modernization plans, the volume of fish landed by the French fishing fleet tripled (Chaussade and Corlay 1988, 31, 51). However, as catching capacities increased and fishing technology improved, job opportunities decreased. In Brittany, the number of jobs plummeted from 25,000 in 1950 to 8,000 in 1992. Today, the catching capacity of Brittany's highly capitalized and efficient artisanal fishing fleet greatly exceeds the reproductive capacity of the fish stocks (Salz 1991; Gwiazda 1993). As we saw above, in a desire to minimize social disruption among fishers while simultaneously attempting to conserve fish stocks, national and European government agencies introduced a variety of restrictive policies. These measures, however, only compounded the problems of those who fish.

Fish prices in the south Bigoudennie fluctuate depending upon the time of year. All Saints Day (1 November) heralds the beginning of the lucrative holiday season. Fish prices climb to the annual high point as French consumers flock to their local fish counters in preparation for the expansive meals that mark the Christmas and New Year holiday season. The relative scarcity of fish at this time of year works in concert with heightened demand to drive up prices. Consumer demand falls off dramatically in January, driving prices down to what is normally the annual low in the price cycle. The situation is made more difficult since the weather in January and February is the worst of the year. The bad weather keeps most of the under-24-metre vessels tied up to the dock. In the 12- to 18-metre class of vessels, ships' logs indicate an average of 50 per cent of the available fishing days are lost in these months due to poor weather. With the milder spring weather, fish prices start to climb back up slowly. Prices peak during the summer **langoustine** fishery, then drop off a bit in early fall until the holiday rush begins to propel them skyward again.

During the heyday of the artisanal fishing boom in the 1980s, the retail sector in the regional commercial centre, Pont L'Abbé, grew at a remarkable rate while many other rural communities in France were losing their small commercial centres. At the peak of the boom, this small town of 8,000 (servicing an area population of between 30,000 to 35,000 residents) supported more than 200 commercial businesses. A local building boom, propelled by rising fishing incomes, swept the region as fishers replaced old buildings with larger, modern homes in the interior of the region. The new homes were more reminiscent of the cannery owners' homes of an earlier era than of the small, cramped homes of their parents. Following four to five generations of hard times, it seemed to the fishers that the good times had finally arrived. Little luxuries that had been denied their parents and grandparents became a normal aspect of everyday life. Growth and expansion seemed unending. The drop in overall production that had begun in the mid-1980s was more than offset by steadily rising prices. For many, the crisis of the early 1990s came as a complete shock.

Early warnings of crisis were apparent in 1992. Falling catches combined with declining prices made that a poor year for the majority of the ports in the Bigoudennie. The precipitous drop in fish prices was the by-product of two unrelated economic changes. The first was a currency crisis in which the Italian, Spanish, and British currencies devalued relative to the French franc. This affected Bigouden fishers in two ways. First, close to 60 per cent of locally caught fish is sold on the Spanish and Italian markets; a drop in those currencies had a direct impact on the price of fish in Le Guilvinec. Second, British fish enters in sizeable enough quantities to have a major impact on the price of fish in the Spanish market. The second major economic change was the liberalization of import regulations affecting fish products. EU policies introduced in 1992 simultaneously allowed fish from non-member states (specifically from the Americas and Africa) into the EU market and cut minimum price supports. The impact of these economic changes made the decline in fish catches even more apparent and the crisis that much more severe.

Overall production fell by 7.2 per cent (72,123 metric tons versus 77,728 in 1991). The registered value of the catch dropped by 5.7 per cent (1.3 million francs against 1.4 million in 1991). In the Bigoudennie, the 1992 crisis had a variable effect. Declines in overall production ranged between 8 per cent and 11 per cent. The aggregate price per kilo of fish dropped by 23 per cent in January 1993. While the magnitude of the drop was unusual, it was not unexpected to experience a drop in prices during the first few sales of the new year. However, prices continued dropping throughout 1993; indeed, they were in free fall until spring/summer 1995 when they stabilized at 15 per cent less than the 1991 pre-crisis price. The impact on the local economy was devastating.[1]

DAYS OF PROTEST

During the holiday season of 1992, prices did not climb nearly as high as was expected, and when the January price drop arrived, it hit with the force of the famed French high-speed train. Gentle pre-Christmas warnings by the president of the local fishers' committee in its bulletin were quickly transformed into a general protest movement that at its peak stretched along most of France's Atlantic coastline. The movement had its roots in the government-mandated local committees of fishers (CLPM), but as the nature of the protest changed from lobbying to direct action, informal "survival" com-

---

[1] Affaires Maritimes, Le Guilvinec. Annual Reports 1991–95.

mittees sprang up and soon displaced the official committee structure as the effective political voice. The local committees established by the French state in 1945 are part of a well-integrated and centralized management system that brings together all sectors of the French fishing industry under one umbrella organization, the **Comité national des pêches maritimes et des élevages marins** (CNPMEM). Although they have a certain degree of autonomy, they are ultimately responsible for the "execution of decisions taken at a higher level" (Salz 1991, 137; for discussion of an analogous management system in Spain, see LiPuma and Meltzoff 1994).

It is important to point out that in spite of the new structure and separate organization, many of the CLPM personnel were also involved in the organization and leadership of the survival committees, which in many instances were run out of the CLPM offices and were funded by the official organization. Unhampered by government bureaucracy and rising out of local networks of co-operation and **kinship**, the survival committees were able to mobilize large numbers of fishers, family, and community members in a relatively short period of time.

With few exceptions, the Bigouden skippers participated in the mobilization. The majority of the organizing committee members were also skippers. The two leading members of the survival committee, André Le Berre and Dominique Lepart, are skipper-owners of vessels in the 24-metre class. In addition to being a member of the survival committee, Le Berre was also a member of the nominally left-leaning union, the Confédération générale du travail (CGT), and was president of the CLPM.

Four thousand demonstrators marched through the streets of Le Guilvinec on 22 February 1993, the day before Breton fishers stormed the Rungis fish market. The newspaper *Ouest-France*[2] declared: "In the memory of the Bigoudennie, we haven't seen so many people demonstrating in Le Guilvinec since May '68." Survival committee organizers declared the demonstration a success: "Here, everyone understood that if the fishery crashes, everyone will crash along with it"[3] (O-F, 23 February 1993). The exasperation and anger of the demonstrators were reflected in the slogans on their placards: "**Briezh** fish inside, American fish outside"; "Brussels—watch the cauliflower and leave us the fish"; "Fish unsold, Fishermen in rags"; "US Go Home." The speakers stood on a makeshift platform draped in the black and white of the Breton flag and the orange and yellow of the Bigouden flag. In a manner

---

[2] 23 February 1993. All future references to *Ouest-France* will be listed in text as follows: (O-F, day month year); my translation.

[3] My translation.

evocative of an English-Canadian unity rally or a St. Jean Baptiste celebration in Québec, these visible signs of the Bigoudennie and the Breton swayed through the demonstration and in the words of the speakers. While simultaneously recognizing, even supporting, the need for an effective pan-European fishing policy, speaker after speaker referred to the community base of the fishery and the importance of the fishing industry in economic and cultural terms.

The Bigoudennie was the epicentre of the protest. A careful plotting of direct actions and demonstrations set against the landscape of France's Atlantic coast dramatically illustrates the central role of this place in the uprising that swept through the French fishing industry (Couliou 1994, 11–12). Roving bands of fishers entered grocery stores and cold-storage facilities and destroyed thousands of kilos of imported fish. Trucks loaded with imported fish were held up on local highways and their contents dumped out. The national government tried to put out the flames of protest with the promise of a 225-million franc "emergency plan" and an offer to review government fisheries policy (*Le Télégramme*, 24 February 1993). The protests continued unabated.

As spring weather gradually replaced the meanness of winter storms, however, the daily necessity of earning a living slowly took over. Sporadic direct actions occurred well into June, but modest price increases over the summer and during the 1993 holiday season kept the fishers at sea. Government largesse also allayed the concerns of some boat owners, especially those most in difficulty who were promised financial assistance. The basic problem, however, remained as before, and in January 1994 protest erupted again.

In 1993, the skippers had been at the forefront of the struggle. In 1994, crewmembers tried to push their demands on working conditions and pay into the limelight without much success. At a general meeting of all fishers in Le Guilvinec, organized by the survival committee, a call was issued for a general strike of all artisanal fishers. Most of France's Atlantic fishery was shut down for the better part of February. As in 1993, the fishers organized roving bands of "commandos" whose task it was to destroy imported fish wherever it was found. Other units went into the local markets to hand out copies of the prices fishers received at the dock. Local town councils worked with the survival committees to organize "dead city days" in which all the merchants of the town closed their shutters in support of the fishers (and incidentally avoided attacks by units of commandos).

The national government acted quickly to forestall an escalation of the protest. In answer to the strike organizers' demands, a meeting was set up in Rennes, the capital of Brittany, between then-prime minister Eduard Bal-

FIGURE 1.3: Fishers tossing out imported fish at a cold-storage facility

ladur and elected CLMP representatives.[4] On the day of the meeting, several thousand fishers, their families, and supporters demonstrated outside. While the prime minister talked with the fishers, riot police chased demonstrators through the streets of the city using tear gas, rubber bullets, and clubs. The fishers fought back with distress flares, one of which landed on the roof of the historic former parliament building of Brittany.

Early the next morning, demonstrators returned home to pictures in the local newspapers of the burning building and fishers with bloody and beaten faces. The burning of the parliament building dampened community support a little. Yet, despite this momentary setback and the beginnings of vocal criticism at home in the Bigoudennie, fishers continued their protests in Rennes until the government promised more subsidies to help boat owners in difficulty. Crewmembers, however, received little attention. Social cleavages at the local level between skipper and crew started to widen and made subsequent solidarity more difficult. One of the outcomes of this was the growth of a new union, the Force Ouvrière (Workers' Force), on the 24-metre vessels based in the Bigouden port of Loctudy.

The lacklustre conclusion of the 1994 phase of the social protest reflected the internal contradictions of the fishing communities themselves and reveals a contrasting and antagonistic set of social interests between skipper and crew. I will return to this in Chapter Four, but for now it is enough to say that in promoting their own social interests, the boat owners relied upon the simultaneous support and subordination of their crews.

THE IMPACT OF THE CRISIS ON EVERYDAY LIFE

Under capitalism, conservation and resource management practices almost always take into account maintaining the best rate of profit over the medium to short term. In the case at hand, moreover, conservation plans have been designed outside the community of fishers and are oriented toward fulfilling needs and objectives that have very little to do with the local community (Rogers 1995; Stump and Batker 1996). For their part, members of the local community are pulled inexorably into a vortex of increasing capacity and diminishing returns until the fishery collapses completely. Local people are then forced to either switch to a new fishery or be pushed out of fishing forever.

In the Bigoudennie, the direct impact of the crisis on the fishing fleet was reflected in the day-to-day operations of the fishing boat in three specific

---

[4] Most of the representatives who met with Balladur were boat owners.

respects: reductions in crew size, reductions in expenditures on maintenance of vessels, and increased fishing time. In combination, these responses resulted in a worsening of shipboard safety. For example, since 1989 the crew size on a fleet of 24-meter boats belonging to one local fishing company declined from six to five at sea. During the same period, many of the coastal draggers went from four to three men at sea.[5] Whereas technological changes (such as the switch from side-trawling to stern-trawling) were at the root of downsizing crews in the past, in the mid-1990s the explanation is directly economic. Fewer men in the crew translates directly into bigger crew shares of declining income.

Many boat owners also cut back as much as possible on maintenance expenditures. Boats were taken up on the slipway less frequently than was previously the practice. Gear was made to last longer than usual, and the replacement of old equipment was deferred, often beyond the point of safety. In the short run, this form of economizing improved the productivity of the vessels and thus increased the boat owners' revenue and (perhaps) maintained or at least slowed down declining incomes. However, over the long term these measures led to a deterioration of conditions of work and a worsening of shipboard safety.

The crisis also had a social and economic impact on fishers' families. Most obviously, declining incomes forced changes in the management of the household budget. In confronting "the perennial problem of the peasantry" (Wolf 1966), fishing families had little recourse but to increase production (that is, to fish longer and harder) and to restrict their consumption on the fishboat and in the household. Changes in patterns of household spending had a serious impact on the local retail economy. However, it was the hidden processes of economizing and their impact on the fishers' families that underlay much of the widespread anger and spurred the Bigoudennie to protest.

Until the crisis in 1993, Danielle,[6] a mother of two children aged five and two, did not have to work outside of the home. "My husband," she said, "is

---

[5] These data were collected from a variety of sources during my fieldwork in 1994–95, including interviews with fishing skippers and government officials, as well as government reports. I conducted a boat-to-boat survey in which I counted the crews of over half of the vessels in the 12- to 24-metre range. None had crews greater than five on the deep-sea vessels and four on the inshore.

[6] All names are pseudonyms with the exception of those of prominent members of the fishing community, government officials, or elected politicians, quoted by name from published sources. I met Danielle, Nicole, and Françoise at a local food bank run by one of the local Fishermen's Wives Associations. During my stay in the Bigoudennie, I spent a great many hours listening to the women talk about the difficulties of running a household and, for the skippers' wives, keeping the boat accounts during the period of crisis.

away from home 15 days at a time on a dragger in the Irish Sea. His feet barely touch the ground before he's back out fishing.... Since the crisis he has brought home a salary of between 800 and 2,500 francs (US$175–500), typically about 1,000 francs." Until the start of the crisis, Danielle did unpaid labour in her home, including work on her husband's boat accounts. When the crisis hit, she unsuccessfully tried to find employment in the region's service economy. When it deepened, she joined the local Fishermen's Wives Association.

"You think about it," continued Nicole, a mother of three children. "With a sum like that one can't make the house payments or pay the various bills that arrive. I can't properly care for my children anymore, in particular the youngest who is 18 months and has bronchitis."

"What's more, our men love their *métier* and it's not a question of doing something else," said Françoise. "They are worried and on edge because of these financial difficulties and the crisis about which one can see very little to do. Their anxiety affects us and our children. We are worried when we watch them head out to sea, but not as much as when they leave to join the demonstrations. It is a desperate time, and we worry when we hear news of men being arrested and beaten by the police."

"On what do we live?" asked Nicole. "That's the real question. You can ask us, why don't you get a job? But there is no work in this region. Each time we get a bill, we have to go to the bank and negotiate. You know, that is not normal. Our husbands spend 18 hours working each day at sea and make next to nothing. Do you think they'll go begging, cap in hand?"

Due to the nature of the regional economy and high levels of unemployment, it was difficult for fishing families to supplement their losses from fishing with income generated by other family members not already working. The distribution and allocation of paid employment in the Bigoudennie reflects a pattern of gendered employment opportunities common in France and other countries with similar economic structures during this period, with women disproportionately represented in the generally lower-paid portions of the service sector (retail and clerical jobs) and men employed in managerial activities, trades, and fisheries. The retail sector appears now to be at its peak employment level, and, given the region's economic reliance on the fishery, it is unlikely to be able to expand to absorb additional labour.

NEO-LIBERAL GLOBALIZATION AND SOCIAL CONFLICT

Class struggle in the Bigoudennie has shifted decisively, not into obscurity, but out of the tangible arenas of the locality and into the phantasmagorical world of **neo-liberal globalization**. In *Globalization and the Decline of Social Reform*, Gary Teeple paints an exceedingly gloomy picture of the "coming tyranny: ...largely unfettered by political considerations, [it] is a tyranny unfolding—an economic regime of unaccountable rulers, a totalitarianism not of the political sphere but of the economy" (1995, 151). It is against this mature form of capitalism—"late" capitalism—that the boat owners and crews were protesting.

It is critical to place the fishers' struggle within the context of the state. How does the nature of the state create and/or restrain the possibility of social action? Is the state neutral in social conflicts? If the Breton fishers' protest movement suggests anything, it is that the state is not neutral. We therefore need to carefully consider the nature of the state and its role in regulating the economy. In addition, there are two particular aspects of the fishers' protest that bear closer examination: the structural features of the local matrix of class forces and the particular tactical approach employed by the fishers. I will consider each in turn.

THE STATE

At its most simplistic, the state within a capitalist economy is an executive committee of large business interests. The contemporary state has (or, in the case of the EU, nation-states have) a critical role in facilitating the smooth accumulation of capital with a minimum of social disruption. The state has at its command the exclusive control of coercive force (police, army, law, etc.) and effective redistributive powers with which it is able to underwrite the infrastructural costs of production (building roads and airports, for example). However, the state is not simply the adjunct of a ruling class; it is simultaneously a product of the historical development of capitalism *and* an actor in the process itself. Two common views of the state are (1) the state as external to or autonomous from the economic system, and (2) the state as capital. Both these views tend to obscure the actual relationship between the state and capital. On the one hand, they allow the state too much autonomy; on the other, they accord too much dependency of the state on capital.

In the state-as-autonomous model, the state is seen "as external to the capitalist economic system. Capitalism in this view, consists in the pursuit of profits by firms (or, more accurately speaking, the self-expansion of capitals) without regard to where they are based geographically. The state, by contrast, is a geographically based political entity, whose boundaries cut across the operation of individual capitals" (Harman 1991, 3). This implies that there is a separation between the political and the economic. Thus, the struggle against police violence, for example, is seen not as a problem intrinsic to capitalism but rather as a separate political or even ethical issue.

The state-as-capital model has its intellectual roots in the writings of the classical Marxist theorists Lenin (1934) and Bukharin (1929). Of special note are their descriptions of the state merging with capital, which they call state monopoly capitalism or state capitalism, and which has often been used to describe Soviet-style communism (Cliff 1988). However, to argue that "every state acts at the behest of a set of nationally based capitals, and every significant capital is incorporated in a particular state" (Harman 1991, 5) is to take the state-as-capital model too far.

According to Harman, "the implications of the view of the state and capital as merging completely are just as great (as in the state as superstructure [or autonomous]). The forms of oppression maintained by the state are seen as flowing directly from the accumulation needs of capital. … The consequence of such a view is to drop any distinction between fundamental social clashes which challenge the very basis of capitalist rule and less fundamental ones that can be contained by reforms to the existing institutional structure" (1991, 6). The end result is a "movement-based" coalition politics in which class is seen as merely one of several possible sites of struggle rather than the primary site. The fundamental basis of the relationship between state and capital is best understood in terms of the concrete ways in which they interact in the course of historical development: "Existing national states did arise out of the developing capitalist organization of production as superstructures. But they feed back into that organization, helping to determine its tempo and direction" (7).

The logic of capitalist development leads to the concentration and rationalization of capital. Within this process, the nation-state becomes "the nodal point around which capitals cluster, even when their activities lead them to branch out from it to penetrate the rest of the world" (Harman 1991, 22). This trend toward the conjoining of state and industry began in the late nineteenth century, but it did not reach its fullest development until the 1930s, when individual "private capitals seemed incapable of recovery from economic crisis if simply left to their own devices" (23). Thus emerged the period of state capitalism, represented in the West by the welfare state and in the East by Soviet-style communism (bureaucratic state capitalism). These two forms are variants on a common theme and have important implications for the manner through which social struggles manifest themselves.

The welfare state performs two primary functions: (1) it intervenes in the economy in terms of the "level, distribution, and pattern of consumption" (Gough 1979, 46); and (2) it intervenes "in the process of reproducing labour

power and maintaining the non-working population" (49). These two functions relate to a particular and enduring problem within any capitalist social
formation: overproduction. In fisheries, overproduction leads to a further
complication—depletion of fish stocks. In this context, the state plays a contradictory role of facilitating the accumulation and smooth functioning of
capital accumulation on the one hand while trying (often without success)
to restrict harvesting of fish in a manner contrary to the internal logic of
capital accumulation.

THE CLASS MATRIX

Any one description of class structures is bound to become mired in the
different, conflicting, and contradictory individual locations of class. The
core set of class relations in the Bigoudennie since the collapse of the industrial
sardine fishery in the 1930s is that between skipper and crew. Spinning outward from this core relation is a dizzying array of conflicting and crosscutting
class structures.

The antagonistic class relations between skippers and crews is, to a certain
extent, held in check by kin relations onboard the boats. As I have suggested
elsewhere (Menzies 1992, 88–89; Menzies 1990), a certain degree of egalitarianism permeates the relations onboard small- to medium-scale vessels. This
is partly a by-product of the necessity to co-operate in the sailing and fishing
processes and the familiarity bred of living together for extended periods in
close quarters. While this is by no means to suggest that skipper and crew
live harmoniously and without dispute, it does represent a different form
of class struggle than one that pits an industrial owner against a wage
employee.

In the ancillary industries such as machine and engine repairs, boat building, electronics, fishing-gear manufacturing, and fish processing, small shops
with fewer than 15 employees are the norm. Here, the nature of working in
close physical and social proximity also mitigates against a politics of intense
class conflict.

The agricultural rural economy was, by the 1960s, essentially non-existent
in the coastal strip of southern Bigoudennie and much reduced in the centre
and north of the region. Changes resulting from the EU's Common Agricultural Policy and the domestic French policy help bolster a local dairy
industry, so farming is profitable for those fortunate enough to hold dairy
quotas.

By the 1990s, the structure of social class in the Bigoudennie incorporated
a large white-collar class closely linked to national trade unions and politics
and a private sector dominated by artisanal social relations in which explicit

class-conflict models of struggle had become more memory than reality. A further complication to this picture has been the growth of holiday or secondary housing in the region, especially along the coast. Secondary housing represents between 30 and 50 per cent of the housing stock in the coastal communes.

One further but crucial new factor must also be taken into account. During the period of class struggle in the early years of the twentieth century, **socially necessary labour time** was determined by the regional and national average. The crucial shift, a shift that has served to undermine the economic viability of fishers more than almost any other single factor, is to a world average of socially necessary labour time. The consequences of a global average are similar to the previous consequences of a national average: "a pressure to equalize the conditions of production and exchange and rates of profit, but now on a world level; and a movement towards world prices and world wages" (Teeple 1995, 68). For fishers in Western Europe or North America, it equals real dollar prices at the lowest level in nearly 30 years. The difficulty for fishers at the local level is in trying to "grab hold" of this new faceless reality.

TACTICS OF STRUGGLE

When one faces an invisible foe, it may well feel as though struggle is futile. The tactical approach employed by the Bigouden fishers in the early 1990s simultaneously locked them in an old pattern of demonstration and strike while they tried to find a new form of struggle effective in a world in which the price of fish in Senegal or New England had as much of a bearing on their livelihood as the local system of marketing or government subsidy.

Two components of the fishers' tactical response are worth noting. First, the fishers and their organizations worked quickly to make international contacts. Second, they employed a dual campaign of political protest in the national arena and acts of economic sabotage directed against multinational capital and fish-importing firms.

The attempts by the Bigouden fishers to forge international contacts was qualitatively different from, for example, the fundraising trips organized by striking British coal miners in Thatcherite England. As opposed to that union-style tour in which the primary purpose was to organize support and raise funds, the Bigouden fishers recognized that the price paid to the Senegalese had a direct bearing on their income. So one of their first steps was to forge direct links with fishers' organizations in countries importing fish into France and the EU in an attempt to raise fish prices outside of the continent. Other outreach programs were with fishers in Cornwall, Devon, and

FIGURE 1.4: Panellists at the World Forum of Fish Harvesters in Loctudy, France, October 2000

Ireland who were disenchanted with the CFP.[7] The aim here was to enlist the support of other European fishers to change provisions of the CFP to the benefit of local fleets.

Simultaneously, the fishers' groups organized political and direct action plans to impede the flow of fish products into France. In the changed field of class relations, simply going on strike had no direct impact on anybody but the fishers themselves. In order to affect the core of productive relations within the global economy, the Bigouden fishers had to assault the state's infrastructure and disrupt the transport and sale of fish. As the strikes died down, Bigouden fishers increased their efforts to expand their global reach by participating in the organization of the **World Forum of Fish Harvesters** (WFF) and by forging and deepening international linkages with other fishermen's organizations in Africa, North America, and Europe. They saw these efforts as different sides of the same coin of resistance.

In the fall of 2000, I was a participant in the first worldwide constituent assembly of the WFF, held in Loctudy from 2 to 6 October. André Le Berre,

---

[7] For these English and Irish fishing skippers, the CFP acted as a severe brake on their ability to expand their fishing capacity. Their primary grievance was that non-British fleets had larger national quotas in waters that, if they were not members of the EU, would have been British and/or Irish territorial waters.

now president of the regional fisheries council in Brittany, spoke with pride of the organization's accomplishments in bringing together representatives from artisanal fish harvesters' organizations from all around the globe to forge common cause. Seven years after the beginning of the fishing crisis of the 1990s, he and his fellow Bigouden fishers considered the meeting to be a logical outgrowth of their earlier strikes and direct actions. The WFF continues to this day with general assemblies every three to five years.

The linkages formed through the WFF extend to more than the circulation of information or people. They include material collaborations in support of family-based fisheries, such as working with European non-governmental organizations (NGOS) that have intervened in setting the price of fishing rights along the coast of Africa, joint lobbying through the **Food and Agriculture Organization of the United Nations** (FAO) with regards to policies that favour small-scale fisheries, and direct participation at the EU level in coordinated interventions in the ongoing debates over the CFP. These tactical innovations emerged during the days of protest and represented an important break from previous forms of struggle, which had been more closely tied to the local political arena in the Bigoudennie.

CONCLUSION

The tactical advances made by the fishers in the Bigoudennie suggest that struggle is necessary and that gains, however small, can be won. The Bigouden fishers combined direct action tactics against the state with economic strikes against the corporate sector. They quickly realized that their struggle had to extend beyond the local arena to avoid being ghettoized and demobilized by the state.

The response by the Bigouden fishing skippers to their economic decline and the increased regulatory pressure exerted by the French state and the EU was to organize simultaneously within the community and internation - ally. In so doing, they invoked a remembered history of industrial struggle with its roots in a metaphor of community. In the following chapter, I explore this remembered history of local struggle and the social context out of which the current structures of struggle have emerged.

2

SYMBOLS OF STRUGGLE—RED FLAGS, LACE COIFFES, AND SOCIAL CLASS

MAPPED ONTO THE TOPOGRAPHY of the material conditions of daily life, a culture rooted in the local, yet angled against continuous incursions from "outside," emerged in the Bigoudennie. In the early period (1860–1914), the outside was represented physically by French-speaking cannery managers and owners who brought their money and machinery into the Breton-speaking Bigoudennie. Even though they lived among the Bigouden people, their life-ways, dress, and language were ever-present indicators of both their social and economic differences. The early social movements, which emerged in opposition to this new class of owner, were articulated within the language of class and class struggle. They were symbolized by the red flag and the singing of the *Internationale*. Ironically, the symbol that best exemplifies the constructed identity of the struggles of the 1990s, the local lace coiffe, was only barely emergent at the point of these early struggles, its iconic tall lace cylinder appearing in between the First and Second World Wars.

The struggles were rooted in the local. The physical sites of struggle were the canneries and the streets of the local towns. Yet these struggles were universal in terms of their connection to an international working class. In this chapter, I examine two periods of social protest: (1) the period of conflict that emerged in the context of the new industrial sardine fishery, and (2) the apochryphal origins of the lace coiffe in a peasant insurrection of the late 1600s. In the first part of this chapter I will discuss the nature of the strikes through a detailed recounting of two particular incidents—Penmarc'h-St. Guénolé in 1909 and Le Guilvinec in 1914. Second, I will outline the social conditions that formed the material background of these strikes. Finally, I will explore the symbols and "lessons" that this period of social protest bequeathed to the future. In the latter part, I examine the orgin of the local lace coiffe and its relationship to the contemporary political struggle.

STRIKES AND DEMONSTRATIONS

The strikes and demonstrations of 1875–1936 in the Bigoudennie were not isolated events but occurred within a context of expanding working-class militancy on the national stage (Noiriel 1990, 88–95). Union membership, "still under 200,000 in 1890, had risen to around 1 million in 1914" (Magraw 1992, 99). The average length of strikes increased from seven days in 1875 to 21 in 1902 (Noiriel 1990, 89). *La belle époque* was thus a time of struggle and misery, both tied to the development of new forms of industrial production.

TRASHING FISH IN PENMARC'H-ST. GUÉNOLÉ 1909

In the early morning hours of 7 September 1909, a group of about 60 Penmarc'h-St. Guénolé fishers stopped three wagons of tuna on their way to the Landais cannery to protest the canner's refusal to buy their sardines. First the police and then the town mayor asked the fishers to step aside. According to the police report, the fishers calmly held their ground and refused to move.[1] Shortly after, the demonstrating fishers were joined by another 150 from a nearby port, one of whom was carrying the tricolour— the national flag of France. The police report continues, "They rolled up the blue and the white on the pole to form, in this way, a red flag. Next they tipped over one of the cars. They then took hold of the other two and, despite our presence, they continued the strike and threw the tuna into the sea."[2] After this momentary burst of "over-excitement," the fishers are reported to have "calmed down. Nevertheless, we continued to patrol the streets in groups."[3]

The events described in the police reports were republished in newspaper accounts at the time and following the court proceedings concerning six men arrested after the demonstration. The individual voices of the fishers

[1] AD, Quimper: File, 4S 358, "Rapport du Brigadier Vivier sur l'incident survenu le 7 courant à St. Guénolé."

[2] AD, Quimper: File 4S 358, telegram from Penmarc'h-St. Guénolé to the Prefecture in Quimper, 7 September 1909; my translation.

[3] "Rapport du Brigadier Vivier."

do not emerge in the printed record with the exception of a short series of articles reporting on the court case nearly two years later, in which one of the fishers is reported to have said, "I made like the others, I danced on the fish."[4] Much to the chagrin of the police, all six fishers were acquitted.[5]

Rather than capitulate completely, the cannery owner, M. Landais, attempted to meet his production needs by switching to canning locally grown green peas rather than imported fish from other ports. He was not alone in this strategy. During the Sardine Years, between 20 and 60 per cent of the plants were also canning vegetables and tuna, especially during the fish strikes. However, the issue of buying local fish continued to be a vexing problem and source of conflict between the canners and fishing skippers. Additionally, it provided the primary point of conflict between fishers of different ports within the Bigoudennie.

The police reports focused on the "over-excitement" of the crowd and the specific physical acts committed by the fishers against the property of the cannery as observed by the authorities. The reasons or explanations for the fishers' actions were left unsaid. Socio-economic studies conducted by the Prefecture in Quimper, newspaper reports at the time, and the living memory of fishers active in the protests of the 1990s reveal a different picture. From the viewpoint of the fishers, it was the cannery owner who was culpable: he had refused to buy their fish and chose, instead, to import tuna from another port. At the court case, one of the fishers testified "that they feared dying of hunger if the local canneries refused to buy their fish."[6] While Landais saw the fishers' actions as an infringement on his property rights and his ability to conduct business untrammeled by "violence," for the fishers the issue was their very ability to survive. To them, the primary issue was the price paid by the canneries for the fish, as well as the local-first purchasing policy.

From the vantage point of the early twenty-first century, we can pinpoint two underlying causal factors leading to the crisis in 1909: (1) the biology of the sardine, and (2) a particular confluence of global economic processes. In combination, these factors laid the material basis for the crisis in the Breton sardine fishery and, for working people, resulted in a period of 10 to 15 years of abject poverty and social upheaval.

Sardines, pilchards, and herring often exhibit wild fluctuations in terms

---

[4] *La Dépêche de Brest,* 21 January 1911.

[5] AD, Quimper: File, 4M 203, Letter to "Directeur de la Sureté Général, Paris au sujet des incidents de 7 septembre 1909 à St. Guénolé-Penmarc'h: Verdict de la Cour d'Assises de Quimper."

[6] *La Dépêche de Brest,* 21 January 1911.

of stock size and range. Recent research suggests that population size and viability are closely linked to changes in global climatic conditions and oceanic water temperatures. Between 1902 and 1913, sardines "disappeared" from the waters off the coast of Brittany ("disappeared" should here be taken as meaning the stock, such as it was, was not deemed to be of commercial value). Over the course of these ten years, the bulk of the fish rarely moved north of Belle Isle, nearly 100 kilometres to the southeast of the Bigoudennie. To make matters worse, the fish that did move into the Bigoudennie during these years tended to be too small to be profitably canned by the local industry.

The fishers and their families knew that their very survival was threatened. They fought for a price for the few fish they could catch that would allow them to feed and clothe themselves. It was a desperate time. The situation was so severe that, in 1905, the bakers in St. Guénolé threatened to go on strike and close their shops if the Prefecture did not provide aid to the fishers. In a letter to the prefect, the bakers' committee said they could no longer afford to extend credit to the fishers and their families and that "the people will undoubtedly starve without government support."[7] In 1909, the fishers were fighting to maintain control over who could sell their fish to the local canneries and over the minimum price they would be paid. They had arranged a deal with the canneries in the area, but Landais refused to buy at the agreed-upon price. On the stand in 1911, one of the fishers testified that "the cannery owners had agreed by contract to pay 7 francs per thousand sardines for the first boats, 5 francs for the second boats, with a maximum of 15,000 sardines per boat. . . . M. Landais had refused to sign the contract, so the fishers decided to demonstrate."[8]

The second issue, concerning who could sell fish to the canneries, was just as crucial as the price paid. This was one of the primary sites of conflict *between* fishers in the different Bigouden ports. Fishers from Île Tudy in the east to St. Guénolé in the west fought to maintain local control of fish sales in their ports. These inter-port conflicts serve to highlight the contradictory notion of there being a unified "Bigouden identity." Over the course of the twentieth century, the "local" has been progressively enlarged to incorporate the entire region as opposed to the village. During the period of the sardine crisis, fishers fought both the canners and each other, simultaneously em - ploying a local and a class identity. Control over sales in the local port led

---

[7] AD, Quimper: File 4S 358.

[8] *La Dépêche de Brest*, 21 January 1911. The same fisher also commented on remarks made by the local mayor who had said to the police, "Do what you want, as long as you do not hurt anyone."

to intra-class conflict, and struggles with the canners relied upon inter-port solidarity.[9]

In order to protect their livelihood at the local level, fishers wanted the canners to agree neither to import fish from other ports nor to buy from boats based in a different port. That is, a Penmarc'h cannery was to buy only from boats that habitually sold their fish and hired their crews in Penmarc'h-St. Guénolé. Landais, however, saw this as a direct infringement of his right of free enterprise and thus refused to buy the local sardines (which he argued were too small to be useful anyway) and chose, instead, to bring in three wagonloads of tuna from outside the Bigoudennie. In the ensuing conflict all of the tuna was unloaded and destroyed by the fishers.[10]

Despite the "local" aspect of this incident, it encapsulates the two primary points of conflict within the fishery: struggle over fish prices and control over where fish could be sold. In the fishers' struggles with capital, these have been the two most important points of contention. As systems of marketing, transportation, and processing have become more and more integrated into a single world economy, the ability of fishers to affect change through strikes or direct actions at the local level has diminished considerably. Yet, even in 1909, the fishers' ability to control the price of fish was next to impossible, even when one considers the great number of strikes in the region. Most of the firms engaged in canning were branch plants or had branch plants operating in an international arena that included Spain, Portugal, and North Africa, all sites in which the price of labour was lower and the supply of sardines more regular than in Brittany.

THE STRIKE AT LE GUILVINEC, 1914

The police files maintained in the departmental archives at Quimper reveal the extent to which the canners and the police expected resistance from fishers and cannery workers during the sardine fishing season of 1914. The canners were attempting to rationalize production through the introduction of new processing machinery, a change in the system of purchasing sardines, and by closing certain canneries.

The canners co-operated with the police and provided detailed maps and plans of their canneries along the Breton coastline. In the file for Le Guilvinec, the maps of the five local canneries are titled "*plans de protection*" and indicate where the police were to be located during a strike or protest situation. The

---

[9] For details see AD, Quimper: File 4S 358.
[10] As an aside, several crates of tomatoes in the wagons survived the demonstration unharmed. The fishers carefully unloaded the tomatoes, set them aside, and then proceeded to destroy the tuna.

files list numbers of police (on horse or foot) regularly based in Le Guilvinec and the number and location of potential reinforcements. Essentially, these files document a state–business coalition contingency plan to break strikes should they occur.

The 1914 strike began in the port of Concarneau and rapidly spread along the coast. The canners, represented by a national syndicate, locked out the fishers in Concarneau on 15 June and maintained that they would keep them out until the fishers agreed to the canners' price and new conditions of sale. The canners had unilaterally decided to change the selling of sardines from the customary system by the thousand (*au mille*[11]) to sale by the kilogram, claiming that this would give them better means to control their purchases. The fishers, however, argued that the new system created a situation in which the canners could undervalue their catch and thus pay less than they might have in the previous system.

For the duration of the strike, the majority of the canners believed they could profitably substitute peas or tuna for the sardines. The joint police–business plans of protection focused on access routes along which vegetables and fish from outside the region could be imported. It seems that the canners did not expect the predominantly female workforce in the canneries to join the fishers. This is, however, what happened.

The seven-day strike at Le Guilvinec in June 1914 was far more of a threat to the normal operation of business than the incident at Penmarc'h-St. Guénolé. First, it was part of a Brittany-wide strike. Second, it was a co-operative venture between shoreworkers (mostly women from fishing families) and fishers. Within several days of the strike in Concarneau, the call to strike was answered by fishers and cannery workers in Île Tudy, Loctudy, Lesconil, Le Guilvinec, Penmarc'h-St. Guénolé, Audiene, and Douarnenez, effectively shutting down the entire Breton sardine fishery. At the peak of the strike, more than 7,000 fishers and 3,000 cannery workers were out. The extent of support for the strike varied from port to port. Outside of Concarneau, the strongest public manifestation of support came from the fishers and cannery workers in Le Guilvinec.[12]

Until their fellow fishers in Concarneau went on strike, the Guilvinists had seemingly accepted the change in the selling system without much publicly reported opposition. The issue was discussed in a general meeting of fishers on 22 June 1914, when they decided to go on strike in an act of soli-

---

[11] According to the fishers, the sale *"au mille"* had been in use "since time immemorial" (*La Dépêche de Brest*, 24 June 1914).
[12] AD, Quimper: File 4S.

darity with "their comrades in Concarneau." The strike was declared, and
the boats stayed at anchor in port. The regional newspaper commented that
"the population is calm and the mariners speculate phlegmatically along the
quay facing the sea which they have momentarily deserted. . . . for their families
a day of unemployment will be a day without bread."[13]

On the morning of 23 June, the fishers gathered in a local hall to debate
their continued participation in the strike. To strengthen their position, they
passed a motion demanding an end to all work in the canneries until the
canners reverted to the former system. A meeting of cannery workers was
organized immediately. The gathered women, most of them wives, mothers,
daughters, or sisters of the striking fishers, agreed to join the strike until the
former system was re-established. To show their support, they immediately
began a march through the streets of Le Guilvinec.

The demonstrators, followed by children, began their march by serving
notice to M. Guégan, manager of the cannery Delory of Lorient, that no
work would be carried out in his cannery until he returned to buying sardines
by the thousand. The plant manager replied that "he was an employee like
them and must execute his own boss's orders. The women and girls then
shouted: 'Vive **la grève!**' and led the march to the cannery Salles."[14] The
demonstrators entered the cannery and urged their fellow workers to join
the strike. According to police and newspaper reports, the plant was quickly
emptied of all workers, who left the vegetables waiting to be canned to rot.
The new contingent of workers joined the demonstration and they all moved
off to the third of five canneries, the Société Brestoise. The manager, however,
had already taken precautions and locked all the entrances with his workforce
on the inside. The demonstrators banged on the doors and demanded that
they be opened so that they might discuss the strike with their fellow workers.
According to a La Dépêche reporter, the "energetic approach of the special
commissar, who resolutely defended the right to work, was respected" and
the workers stopped trying to break down the doors to the plant.[15] The commissar was less successful, however, in breaking up the demonstrators who
proceeded to set up outside the plant for the rest of the day. The newspaper
reported: "Mischievous children play about their feet while our charming
Bigoudens busy themselves crocheting Irish Lace. 'We do want to strike, but
we won't leave our precious lace' they say."[16] For the reporter, the women's
crocheting was bemusing: while engaged in something ostensibly as serious

[13] La Dépêche de Brest, 23 June 1914.
[14] La Dépêche de Brest, 24 June 1914.
[15] La Dépêche de Brest, 24 June 1914.
[16] La Dépêche de Brest, 24 June 1914.

FIGURE 2.1: "Luttes sociales en Pays Bigouden." Poster by Alain le Quernec depicting the red flag and local lace coiffe in action

as a strike, they chose to pass their time crocheting lace. However, concealed in the apparently innocent act of domestic labour is something far more important that the reporter failed to recognize. According to the detailed socio-economic surveys conducted by the Prefecture each year during the sardine crisis, the sale of lace brought in as much income, if not more, to each family as did a woman's work in a cannery.[17] Thus, the crocheting was more than simply a way to pass the afternoon at a demonstration; the women were earning money to feed their families while attempting to improve their working conditions and pay. Perhaps if the reporter had realized this, he would not have been so amused by what the "charming Bigoudens" were doing.

Fishers and cannery workers joined forces to demonstrate outside of the Salles Cannery early on the morning of 24 June. The cannery was operating behind a barrier of 20 police on horse and half that number on foot.[18] The manager wanted to complete canning the fresh peas that had been left in the plant following the previous day's strike. However, when the demon-

---

[17] AD, Quimper: File 4S 361 Divers, *Rapport sur la crise sardinière du Guilvinec, 16–24 juin 1914.*

[18] *Rapport sur la crise sardinière.*

strators (mostly women) returned to the cannery, he was forced to close the plant and send his workers home. Even after the plant emptied, the demonstrators refused to move. When the police tried to disperse them, the workers fought back by throwing rocks and sand. Two hours later, the workers left of their own accord to attend a meeting.

Representatives of the striking Concarneau fishers and an official of the Fédération des inscrits maritimes (an organization of fishers) addressed an audience of 2,000 people in the streets of Le Guilvinec. Monsieur Gauthier, of the Fédération, talked about the importance of joining the communist union, the CGT: "To win your struggle, you need the union," he told them. "Only together, united in a union will you be able to force the bosses to listen to you." Monsieur Morillon, secretary of the Syndicat des Matelots Pêcheurs de Concarneau, told the Guilvinec fishers that they would be allowed to sell their fish in Concarneau to canners who had broken ranks with the other industrialists. Following the speeches, the local union announced a meeting later in the day to discuss what action to take, given that the Concarneau fishers had agreed to allow the Guilvinec fishers to sell fish in Concarneau until the Guilvinec canners returned to the old system of sales.[19]

In the meeting that followed, the fishers decided to start fishing again and to give 7 per cent of their catch to the strikers. They decided to remain ashore Saturday, 26 June 1914. Sunday would be their first day back to sea. A portion of the fleet would sell in Le Guilvinec to the one canner, Chacun, who had agreed to return to the old system of sales. However, he would purchase only 80,000 sardines (approximately the catch of five to ten boats). The majority of the fleet would sail with their catch to Concarneau and sell to the canners there who had agreed to return to the old system of sale. All these plans, however, were complicated by the events of 25 June 1914.

The day began with a demonstration in front of the Société Brestoise cannery, the only plant in which workers had not joined the strike. The women strikers marched to the cannery with a red flag at the head of their parade. They tried to enter, but the police pushed them back. The Special Commissar of Police sent a runner for reinforcements, and within five minutes 20 additional mounted police were on the scene. During the scuffle, all of the Société Brestoise workers quit working and left the plant, except for the forewoman and her husband. The strikers held their place against the police for two hours, yelling for the forewoman to leave and throwing rocks at the police. When the woman finally left the plant, she was met by a chorus of boos.

According to the Special Commissar, the actions of the women were directly attributable to the influence of the red flag; he "knew there would

[19] *Rapport sur la crise sardinière.*

be trouble as soon as the seditious emblem was raised and, there it was, at the moment the flag was raised, a volley of rocks was thrown at the police."[20] Fearing a continued and escalating level of social turmoil, the police requested additional reinforcements and help from the armed forces.

With the news of the arrival of these reinforcements in Le Guilvinec, the fishers reversed their previous decision to return to a limited fishery. Over the weekend of 26–27 June 1914, 40 soldiers from Quimper and 18 more police officers were added to the 50 or so police already stationed in the town. The fishers met with the local deputy, George Le Bail, who agreed to act on their behalf and ask the prefect to withdraw the armed forces. In return, the officials of the fishers' trade union made a written promise that they would desist from criminal acts during the strike.

Despite their fractured unity, the canners' association declared a lock-out in all of their canneries in western Brittany. However, the canners were unable to sustain co-operation among themselves, and by 11 July 1914 the majority had reverted to the old system of purchases (Guégruen and Le Maitre 1990, 407). The strike had effectively maintained both fish prices and the traditional system of sales. The ability of the fishers to force the canners to accept their demands relied upon the solidarity between cannery workers and fishers, a form of solidarity that may well be more a product of household dynamics than class consciousness.

PUTTING FOOD ON THE TABLE, OR THE MATERIAL CONDITIONS OF EXISTENCE AMONG THE WORKING POOR IN LE GUILVINEC

The actual cost of living and level of income for fishers and their families during the two decades immediately preceding the First World War are difficult to determine in any exact manner. The reports submitted to the Prefecture between 1909 and 1913 variously estimate family budgets based on wages paid by local canneries to their workers and to fishers, surveys of actual household budgets, tax reports, and census data.[21] These reports document extreme variations between different canneries within and between different Breton ports. In addition, there are variations even within a single cannery, reflecting differences between unskilled jobs women could secure versus the skilled ones given to men, long-term core employees versus short-term em - ployees, and differing levels of production.

---

[20] *La Dépêche de Brest,* 26 June 1914.
[21] AD, Quimper: File 4S 360.

In the Bigouden ports, a reliance on sardine, mackerel, and, to a lesser extent, tuna created a highly seasonal fishery in which both fishers and plant workers were unemployed for close to half of the year. Thus, fishing families could not rely solely upon earnings from the fishing season but had to find alternative work during the off-season. Unlike their peasant cousins who could rely on food reserves put by during harvest, fishing households (especially those in Le Guilvinec) had no such opportunities on which to fall back.

In 1912, fishing household incomes ranged from a low of 770 francs to a high of 1,290 francs, or from 130 to 215 francs per working person in the household. More than half of this income was generated during the three or four months of the sardine fishery. How do these household incomes compare with those of other workers in France at the time? According to Lévy-Leboyer and Bourguignon, a Breton worker in 1882 spent between 129 and 282 francs per person per year on food, which suggests that the Le Guilvinec fishers were living very close to the edge. The average daily wages of women and men working in the fish canneries were, respectively, 1.75–2.5 and 3–4 francs per day. This compares poorly with the average daily wage of women in other industrial areas and with male labourers in Paris (Lévy-Leboyer and Bourguignon 1990). An important supplementary source of income for Bigouden households came from women's lacework.

Introduced to the Bigoudennie by a Catholic order of nuns during a fishing crisis in 1903, the "Irish" style of lacework quickly became an important economic activity and was estimated by the Prefecture in 1911 to contribute as much as 5 francs per day to the household budget of local fishing families. Lacework was conducted by all the female members and young boys of the household. Children, starting at about 11 years, were put to work crocheting. The prefect estimated that laceworkers earned 150 francs per year per household; in times of poor fishing, their lacework made it possible to feed their families.

The period between 1900 and 1914 is remembered as one of extreme poverty. In his memoir, *The Horse of Pride* (1978), **Pierre-Jakez Hélias** recalls women with crying children from Le Guilvinec and Penmarc'h-St. Guénolé begging for food during the winter. The struggle to put food on the table took up most of every day, and the strikes that developed during this period emerged out of the anger and sense of injustice fed by hunger. The Prefecture notes that several hundred families left the Bigoudennie in 1909.

SYMBOLS OF THE STRIKES AND DEMONSTRATIONS

A common theme linking the strikes and political actions during the Sardine Years is their reference point in a language of class and struggle and their invocation of highly symbolic markers such as the red flag. In the contemporary period, the strikes of that earlier period themselves have become symbolic. This is not to deny the abject poverty and the real socio-political issues that gave birth to these particular struggles but rather to point out the underlying multiplicity of meanings and the ambivalence with which people entering periods of crisis "conjure up the spirits of the past to their service and borrow from them names, battle cries, and costumes in order to present the new scene of world history in this time-honored disguise and this borrowed language" (Marx and Engels 1969, 398).

The two most pressing symbols of struggle marshalled to the defence of the Bigouden strikers between the late 1880s and the eve of the Second World War were the red flag and the singing of the *Internationale*. The flag led the processions. Singing was a ritualized way of opening both socialist and union meetings—duly recorded by police spies in and among the strikers and observing from the sides.[22] Clearly, these symbolic acts were "read" by the state as provocative; in one instance, all flags but the tricolour were banned from a public parade.[23]

The red flag is fraught with a double nature: it is both "national" in its invocation of the French Revolution and international as the flag of workers' revolution. In both cases, it symbolizes a threat and provocation to the state and was seen by police as a potent inflammatory symbol. During a strike in Le Guilvinec, for example, as we saw above, one police official suggested the very presence of a red flag was instrumental in precipitating an incident of rock throwing in which two police officers were lightly wounded.[24] The red flag is a reminder of the rights of citizenship within the republic, but more fundamentally, it is part of a collective project engaged in creating "something that has never yet existed" (Marx and Engels 1969, 398). And, as Noiriel points out, "the red flag became the badge of highest honour; it became the late nineteenth century's rallying emblem for workers and their struggle

---

[22] I examine the detailed nature of surveillance in an ongoing project funded by the Humanities and Social Science Research Fund, UBC, called "Ethnographies of Violence: Police Reports of Strikes, Meetings, and Demonstrations in the Bigoudennie, France (1900–1939)."

[23] AD, Quimper: File, 4M 162, Manifestations.

[24] *La Dépêche de Brest,* 26 June 1914; Police Report, AD, Quimper: File, 4S 361 Divers.

everywhere, to the detriment of the tricolor flag symbolizing the Republic" (1990, 94).

The singing of the *Internationale* can be "read" (as indeed metropolitan-based academics have sometime done in private conversations[25]) as a misreading of the French by Breton speakers: "en terre nationale" as opposed to "internationale." While it is more likely that this is a contemporary and deliberate *mis*reading, it points to the violence being enacted upon the Breton people. The gibe at their singing in French fails to acknowledge that their first language, Breton, was actively being erased by the national state.

As the passage of time separates the present from the past, the rough edges of memory are rounded off. One's political perspective is no antidote. Both Left and Right (re)construct romantic images of the past with which to fight their battles for the future. As Sider argues in "Cleansing History" (1996), historical renderings have simplified the past in such a way as to paper over real processes of differentiation and struggle. For contemporary Bigoudens, the period of social protest and struggle during "L'épopée de la sardine" (see Boulard 1991; Tillon 1977, 64–82, 84–85) became a potent symbol of solidarity that was mobilized in the context of the protests of the 1990s.

The period between 1905 and 1936, a time when "*on chantait rouge*" (that is, sang in the language of the Left, as reds; see Tillon 1977), has been reworked in the context of the contemporary protests as a romantic era in which the "community" was united in opposition to an exploitative class of owners. This view is part critique of the present and part longing for a past constructed here as a time in which familial ties were strong and community solidarities important. The contemporary rendering of "L'épopée de la sardine" evokes the importance of community and kin-based networks of mutual support and solidarity while acknowledging their decisive opposition to the industrial "outsiders" represented by the cannery owners and managers who lived in their midst but, in a fundamental way, maintained an impassable social distance between themselves and their workers.

The sardine-crisis strikes of fishers and cannery workers are part of a local memory of struggle and resistance that is held up as an example of the Bigouden character. "We are tough," a member of the local fishing committee told me. "We have a long history of standing up for ourselves against outsiders.

---

[25] During one of many meetings over the years with academics not from the Bigoudennie, I was told a series of jokes about its people. Among other comments was this suggestion that illiterate early-twentieth-century Breton-speaking fisherfolk misheard the lyrics as mentioned here.

When our grandmothers marched through the streets in the 1910s and the 1920s they did so with pride. They wore coiffes and carried the red flag high. Today our flag is different, but the struggle is the same. We are fighting for our right to live as we always have, as Bigouden. We are fighting for our children so that they too can be Bigouden."

This "history of struggle" is understood to extend back in time by several centuries. In the following section I continue the journey back in the local historical memory and describe the unique lace coiffe that in the 1990s became the local embodiment of a tradition of resistance.

LACE COIFFES AND INDUSTRIAL WORK

The tall cylindrical coiffe of the Bigoudennie has become the prime symbol (if not caricature) of the region (Segalen 1991, 2). From tourist brochures to union banners, it is an important domain of local identity. The fetishization of the coiffe both as emblem of the contemporary and marker of the exotic reveals the intimate link between the processes of the everyday and the violence of capital.

The origin of the coiffe is a subject of some debate (Duigou 1990; Cornou 1993; Cousiné-Kervennic 1994). One particularly robust local story roots it in a peasant uprising in 1675, "La Révolte des Bonnets Rouges." The historical evidence, such as it is, suggests a far more recent origin (Duigou 1990, 12), linked in popular memory with local sentiments of resistance and struggle. Whatever the factuality of these stories, the crucial point is the manner in which the social violence of capitalism is etched into the cultural matrix through popular costume and memory. In this section, I examine the sociopolitical development of the coiffe and its symbolic relevance within the domain of contemporary social struggles.

THE COIFFE IN ITS PRESENT FORM

The coiffe in its present shape is a tall, white, lace cylinder worn on top of a woman's head. It is, in fact, a rather elaborate headdress composed of bonnet and lace cylinder. The hair is first pulled up into a tight bun on the back of the head, upon which a small, black, cloth bonnet is secured. The lace cylinder is then attached to the bonnet by hairpins, and two lace ribbons are tied under the woman's chin.

The coiffe is normally worn with a plain black dress and shawl. On special occasions (fêtes, cultural and religious events, marriages, etc.) an elaborately embroidered vest and blouse are also worn. The dominant colours of the

FIGURE 2.2: Union banner with cartoon of coiffed Bigoudène

vest are orange and yellow, the colours of the pre-revolutionary Barony of Pont L'Abbé and the contemporary Bigouden flag.

The coiffe appears in three specific socio-symbolic contexts: (1) as a regular item of clothing worn by a dwindling number of elderly women, (2) as a tourist and marketing image, and (3) as worn by young women at special "cultural" events. Given the extent of tourism during the summer months, the dividing line between these three can at times become blurred, as everyday life is transformed into performance. It is not uncommon, for example, to see several elderly women with coiffes in Pont L'Abbé on market day. During the height of the tourist season, one may witness the rather surreal sight of an elderly Bigoudène moving slowly through the market, stopping here and there as she makes her weekly purchases. Her coiffe, visible above the crowds, stands like a lighthouse attracting the turned gaze of tourists, the boldest of whom are busy taking her photo as she passes by. A similar scene replays itself in the heart of the rainy Breton winter, except the cast of thousands is reduced to just the local inhabitants who take no notice of the "old Bigoudène" as she passes by with her coiffe encased in a special clear plastic bag to protect it from the rain and wind.

The coiffe as icon is splashed across a multitude of advertisements, publicity brochures, and tourist knick-knacks. Everyone from the local tourist authority, to the town council of Pont L'Abbé, to a windsurfing school in Loctudy uses it for publicity. My favorite example is a cartoon image of a feisty, muscular Bigoudène who, with her coiffe on top and sleeves rolled up and ready for battle, is pictured on the local CGT's union banner (see Figure 2.2). The annual Fête des Brodeuses in July is held to celebrate local culture (and, not insignificantly, to attract tourists). Part tourist extravaganza and part cultural revival, this parade and cultural festival of embroidery has been slowly growing since its inception in the 1950s, but it exploded in popularity during the 1980s and 1990s.

FIGURE 2.3: Young women in Bigouden coiffes, Pont L'Abbé

Until the late 1950s, most of the women in the Bigoudennie wore a coiffe for all manner of occasions, ranging from work in the canneries and in the home to important public occasions and events. Few, if any, young women coming of age in the 1960s wore it. Coincident with the wider processes of "modernization," the coiffe was seen as retrogressive, traditional in a negative sense, and a marker of inferior social class. Emulation of aristocratic costume was replaced by an emulation of "bourgeois" dress with its attendant under-statement and neutrality (Le Wita 1994, 57–61). Though modelled on an aristocratic costume, the coiffe is every bit as much a product of the twentieth century as are automobiles or assembly-line production.

In the late 1980s, young women whose mothers stopped wearing the coiffe in the 1950s joined folk groups in which they wore the local costume and performed "traditional" folk dances. The growth of the pan-Celtic movement and its attendant folk festivals is not unlike the growth of the pan-Indian powwow movement in North America. Currently, a growing number of young women are choosing to be married in traditional costume and/or to wear the coiffe for their wedding pictures.

In the mid-1800s, the coiffe was little more than a suggestion, a slight peak at the front of an otherwise unremarkable bonnet. The coiffe rose (both literally and figuratively) out of the flux and disruption initiated by the fishery during the early years of the twentieth century. Innovation began among the young women working in the canneries and then spilled inland. The last generation to wear the coiffe as a regular item of clothing was also the last generation to work in the canneries, which closed down in the 1950s. As the canneries left, job opportunities for women shifted into the service sector (retail and government) where the coiffe appeared outmoded and peculiar.

In the 1980s and 1990s, the coiffe re-emerged in folk festivals, pan-Celtic cultural events, and as a marketing icon in the tourist trade. Today the coiffe has lost its link to the everyday and, with the exception of a dwindling group of elderly women, is now worn only as a costume. It is, moreover, an extravagant marker of local identity symbolically linked with an imagined past.

STORIES OF THE COIFFE'S ORIGIN

The symbolic power of the coiffe in the political protests of the 1990s is linked to a particularly enduring story of its origins, a story I was told many times by fishers to explain why it was important to them that their mothers and grandmothers wore their traditional coiffes at demonstrations and protests. The story dates to a late-seventeenth-century peasant revolt called, in the Bigoudennie, the "Revolt of the Red Bonnets." This was part of a more generalized Breton uprising against the imposition of a new tax levied by Louis XIV to finance his ongoing battles with other European states. The specific mechanism was the introduction of a paper stamp that had to be attached to legal documents to indicate that the tax had been paid. In Brittany, the new tax was seen to be an attack on the privileges of the province, "a declaration of hostilities" (Duigou 1989, 3). The revolt began with a riot in Rennes on 18 April 1675 and quickly turned from protest against the tax to an outright rebellion against the feudal system. Peasants sacked the country mansions of the nobility and executed nobles. Peasants in the Bigoudennie entered the fray two months later on 23 June 1675, when Nicolas Euzénou de Kersulaün, Seigneur du Cosquer, was fatally wounded by members of the congregation of the church of Combrit while sitting in his reserved box during a high mass.

The insurgents extended their control over the barony of Pont L'Abbé within three or four days. Escaping them, the local nobility withdrew first to Pont L'Abbé and then to Quimper. On 2 July 1675, the rebels gathered at Notre Dame de Tréminou, a small church in Plomeur, a scant five kilometres from Pont L'Abbé, to proclaim their Peasant Code. It established a popular militia and abolished feudal rights, which were described as "a tyrannical enemy of the freedom of **Amorique**" (Duigou 1989, 31). In the following two months, government troops slowly moved across the Breton landscape putting down resistance. They arrived in force in the Bigoudennie in September 1675 and between 2 and 17 September smashed down the steeples of six local churches that had been used by the insurgents to coordinate their revolt.

According to the historian Serge Duigou, "The most famous legend of the Bigoudennie is the story of the Bonnets Rouges—the red hats. Everyone knows that the dizzyingly tall coiffes of Pont L'Abbé have their origins in the troubles of 1675: 'The Duke of Chaulnes has razed our church steeples? All right,' declared the women of Combrit and Lambourg, 'we shall raise the steeples again on top of our own heads!'" (1989, 19).[26]

Duigou and others are quick to point out the mythic aspect of this story. However, what is important is not so much what actually happened but, rather, the way in which the story roots the coiffe's origin in a moment of peasant revolt against feudalism. As myth, the story reveals a local sentiment of resistance within which gender and class are intertwined. In the present, the story is told as parable, understood as not "actually" real, but "essentially" true in its reference to the power of women, the history of resistance, and the primordiality of local distinctiveness.

In debunking the "myth," two important factors are left untouched: (1) the social context out of which the story appears to have emerged, and (2) the gendered aspect of the story. The first factor speaks to the context of the present, that is, the simultaneous present of the Sardine Years and the social struggles of the early 1990s. The second makes any simple correspondence between class and struggle difficult to sustain without moving into the domain of tension and struggle within as well as between classes.

THE POLITICAL CONTEXT

The coiffe emerged within a period of intense social strife in the Bigoudennie that culminated in the election of the United Front government of 1936. The mass working-class movement was also part of an inescapable process through which a rural peasantry was transformed into a semi-urban proletariat. The seemingly anachronistic, even paradoxical, expression of "tradition" as manifested in the elaboration of the locally distinct lace coiffe must be placed in the context of these processes of social dislocation. As Bryan Palmer points out, "Capitalism does not so much come to the countryside. The backcountry is itself the site of historical transformation, generating social (gender/racial) relations, proto-industrialization, demographic convulsions, and market forms pivotal in the transition to capitalism" (1994, 15). The

---

[26] My translation.

FIGURE 2.4: Bigoudène in coiffe at a demonstration in Le Guilvinec

Bigouden fishery, which in 1900 included 10,000 fishers and 30,000 workers in more than 100 canneries, plus several thousands more in support industries such as net making and boat building, was one space within a wider field of industrialization and social strife.

It is crucial to note that the elaboration of a "traditional" costume was not isolated to the Bigoudennie. Similar processes can be identified throughout the region. In practically all cases, these examples of "cultural innovation" stem first and foremost from young women entering waged employment in industrial food-processing plants, thus simultaneously maintaining and severing their connections with the agricultural-based networks of kin, reciprocity, and exploitation. As Sider notes, such examples of intensifying cultural particularism are directly associated with the elaboration and intensification of locally specific forms of inequality, both within and between communities (1997b).

The coiffe emerged as a symbol of local identity at precisely the moment when the Bigoudennie was undergoing a transition from a rural agricultural society to an industrial capitalist economy, with women economically and metaphorically in the middle, working in canneries and married to skippers and their crews. The structure of social inequality was changing from one in which the primary lines of control over labour were located within the family to an industrial waged economy in which the previous kin-based forms of control were disrupted. The old paternalism of the father was being replaced by a new paternalism in which the patron of the cannery or factory now appropriated the labour power of household members. Given the **division of labour** between men and women, this new form of social inequality had different meanings for the genders. Men working on the fishboats were nominally independent of the direct control of capital over their labour, while women were working under the direct control of capital.

There is a certain irony in the contemporary use of the coiffe as a symbol of resistance and of community solidarity by a group of fisher*men*. The coiffe, as discussed above, emerged at a point in time during which young women were breaking out of the paternalism of the peasant household through their newfound access to waged employment. For these young women, the coiffe was a modern statement of wealth, independence, and their sexuality. Yet, in its contemporary adaptation as a cultural marker, it appears as a nostalgic emblem of past moments of resistance. The coiffe becomes an icon of "groupness" in the face of an increasingly globalized social world.

CONCLUSION

Red flag and lace coiffe entered the symbolic lexicon of the Bigouden people through their struggle to assert and maintain their everyday livelihood. Contemporary activists deployed references to memories of past struggles, captured in the image of the red flag, as they mobilized their fellow fishermen and neighbours. These were not invented struggles—many families in the region shared the memories of the hard times of the sardine years. The lace coiffe marks off the region as being different, a symbol of a local identity. It also shares with the red flag a memory of struggle and resistance; even in the face of repression and the destruction of their village churches, the Bigouden women took action and raised the church steeples atop their own heads!

PART TWO

THE MATERIAL CONDITIONS
OF THE EVERYDAY

From his rocky height he looked in leisurely fashion over the rich kingdom of Rockbound, where, from land loaded with sea dung and fish entrails, hay, potatoes, strawberries, and vegetables of all kinds grew in profusion. The island, elliptical in shape, was but a mile long and perhaps a half mile wide in its widest part, and consisted of two rounded spruce-clad knolls, at eastern and western ends, with a cleft between them. In the northern end of this cleft or shallow valley stood the fish houses and dwellings of Jungs and Krauses. Throughout the valley, from sea to sea, were fields of rank timothy and rich garden plots of growing potatoes and cabbages. Two of the hills on the western end had been cleared and turned into hayfields, and named respectively Crook's Hill and Wilson's Hill, after two old pioneers who had broken their hearts in the clearing, and gone back to the mainland bent old men defeated by cold, hardship, and the savage sea. In rough weather, when winter seas broke on the southern bar, spray and blown spume flew clear across the valley to the northern shore. Always the sea snarled and gnawed at the bar.   —Frank Parker Day, *Rockbound* (1928)

FOR MUCH OF THE TWENTIETH CENTURY, anthropologists cut their teeth doing fieldwork in small, remote, rural communities such as the fictional Nova Scotian island community of Rockbound. This began to change in the latter half of the twentieth century when a wave of national liberation struggles, beginning with China and India and then spreading across Asia, Africa, and Latin America, forced anthropologists to ask hard questions about such studies. By the end of the century, they were as likely to conduct their fieldwork in Western Europe or North America as they were in Asia or Africa.

The changing venue for research has not lessened anthropological interest in learning about how people navigate their daily world. Whether one studies a traditional fishing village in Nova Scotia or the contemporary fishing ports of the Bigoudennie, there is a need to understand how the everyday works. In the first part of this book, the politics of survival in the Bigoudennie was discussed in terms of three specific moments of organized resistance—the days of protest and attempts at organizing global responses in the 1990s, the Sardine Years of 1880–1930, and the period of peasant resistance in the 1700s— and the attendant symbols employed in those struggles. In Part Two, we move from the images and memories invoked through struggle to consider the material conditions of everyday life out of which the political movements emerged.

Day-to-day conditions, tasks, cycles, and responsibilities are mundane and repetitive. Yet they are simultaneously the terrain within and upon which struggles for survival are inscribed: here is the site of anguish and terror, fear and love. These sites of the everyday are what make the politics of survival worthwhile and give meaning to the construction of local identity. The flying of red flags at the head of a march and the majesty of the lace coiffe are the distilled manifestations of life lived moment to moment.

After first locating the contemporary moment within its historical context, an episode of industrial capitalism in a resource-extraction hinterland, in the following chapters I examine the gendered worlds of work of men and women. This movement from boats, to stories of women and about women, and then to the work experiences and histories of men and women in the Bigoudennie is the critical background against which the struggle of the Bigouden family-based fishing enterprises is enacted. It is this everyday world of fishboats, children, accounting, shopping, and the myriad other details of normal life that gives meaning to ordinary people's struggles.

3

EPISODE, NOT EPOCH: BUILDING CAPITALISM IN THE HINTERLAND

THE INSPIRATION FOR THE TITLE of this chapter comes from Eric Hobsbawm's essay "Industrialization: The Second Phase 1840–95." In reference to working-class acceptance of capitalism, he wrote, "Contrary to the apologists of the system, it [capitalism] offered them little even in theory, at any rate, so long as they remained workers—which most of them were destined to do. Until the railway era it did not even offer them its own permanence. It might collapse. It might be overthrown. It might be an episode and not an epoch" (1969, 123). While the empirical details and actual situation that Hobsbawm describes are undeniably different, for working classes in the south Bigoudennie, industrial capitalism has in fact been more episode than epoch. The area is part of capitalism's "backcountry," a region that sits idle or ignored until colonized by capital or completely abandoned.[1]

The birth of the fishing industry in the Bigoudennie was accompanied by a profound social transformation whose corollary was the near total disappearance of agriculture. Prior to the emergence of the **industrial fishery** of the late 1880s, economic development was held in check by a set of **social relations of production** in the peasant community that relied on containing labour power within the family. The coastal people employed a variety of subsistence strategies as part of their survival kit, among which was an inshore

---

[1] See, for example, Bryan Palmer's (1994) description of the arrival of Goodyear in the backcountry of Ontario, Canada. What is important in Palmer's analysis is that regions that seem to be outside the normal orbit of industrial capitalism are crucially located as potential reserves of both "space" and labour. In the case of Goodyear, the relocation of its tire plant out of an industrial urban setting (Toronto) into the countryside served the corporation in terms of undermining worker organization in Toronto and extracting concessions in a backcountry area starved for jobs.

dinghy fishery. Growing population in the late 1800s increased pressure on the local peasant economy, which was unable to absorb the surplus labour power. The impetus for change was development in the national economy. The growing network of railways (spurred on by industrial interests) finally reached Quimper in 1863 and Pont L'Abbé in 1872. Capital investment in physical plant followed quickly. The implantation of industrial capital in the Bigoudennie broke the bonds of peasant social relations and set the stage for the region's brief flirtation with industrial capitalism. Crucial to this process was the existence of a potentially surplus labour force and the growing metropolitan demand for cheap food products to feed France's northern industrial workforce.

FROM PEASANT TO WORKER

The pre-1880s peasant agriculture in the Bigoudennie had stagnated under the stress of social relations tied to a peasant system of production locked into "tenant farming and an egalitarian system of transmitting goods" at the point of generational succession (Segalen 1984, 130; see also Segalen 1991). By the late nineteenth century, growing population increased the pressure on the local peasant economy to such an extent that out-migration was the only alternative for many. However, the development of a commercial fishing industry completely transformed the area's social and economic structure. According to Segalen, "The crisis in agriculture ought to have resulted in a mass exodus from the countryside at the end of the nineteenth and the beginning of the twentieth centuries. However, this was deferred for thirty years by the growth of fishing and related activities" (Segalen 1991, 234; see also Vauclare 1985, 15).

Surplus labour is "is necessarily a 'relative' concept, and a surplus only exists in relation to a given type of production system" (Nun, cited in Worsley 1984, 188). Before the arrival of the sardine canneries, one cannot truly talk of a reserve army of labour in the Bigoudennie waiting to be called into service. The form of agricultural production there relied on human (not machine) labour, and little progress had been made toward agricultural intensification. According to Segalen, "demographic pressure militated against any kind of technological innovation" (1991, 224). The introduction of machinery at the end of the nineteenth century occurred in the context of the development of the sardine industry. The possibility of replacing agricultural workers with machinery and thereby creating "surplus labour" emerged out of the transition to industrial capitalism within the local economy.

The primary limiting factor for the development of the fishing industry was the lack of adequate and accessible rail linkages between the Bigoudennie and Paris. Investment in transportation infrastructure by the state and private enterprise, and in sardine factories by private capital, rapidly transformed the local economy.[2] In the space of less than ten years, Le Guilvinec jumped in population from a small hamlet of fewer than 200 to over 6,000 people working in the canneries and on the fishboats.

During this "episode" of industrialization (1880–1950), the face of coastal Bigoudennie was fundamentally altered. Involvement in the industrial waged economy was crucial for more than half of the 30,000 people living within the southern portion of the Bigoudennie. A report to the Prefecture in 1913 described a "typical" household as one that included six family members earning income from industrial sources. While one may speculate that some form of subsistence practice was used to supplement the household budget, the report unambiguously states that the people living in the newly urbanized coastal strip no longer engaged in any form of agriculture.

The primary impetus toward economic development came in the form of the investment of industrial capital based in metropolitan France. Railroads created an opportunity for capital investment to access the resident labour pool and, in the process, remade the local population into a Bigouden working class. The first step was the extension of joint state- and private-funded rail links into the Bigoudennie. Quimper, the regional capital, was linked with the markets of Paris by rail in 1863. A regional spur line linked the Bigoudennie with Quimper (and thus to Paris) in 1884. While it is alluring to see the railway as being the causal factor in the phenomenal growth of the sardine fishery in the Bigoudennie (within two years of the establishment of the rail head in Quimper, five sardine canneries were established; by 1901, 20 canneries were operating), the development of the railway should not be seen in isolation from the metropolitan-based food industry or the local-level political leadership's economic aspirations. The expansion of the rail links into the region was pursued as a development strategy and, as such, was a product of the wider processes of industrial development in France at that time.

The growth of the sardine fishery in the south Bigoudennie was part of a larger development of the sardine fishery that followed the invention of the canning process in the 1840s in Nantes. This new technique for preserving

---

[2] For an interesting discussion of railways and their importance in the development of "second phase" industrial capitalism, see Hobsbawm 1969, 109–33; for their role in turning "peasants into Frenchmen," see Weber 1976, 195–220; and for a comparison of British, American, and French approaches to the construction of railways, see Dobbin 1994.

fish revolutionized the fishing industry and, combined with assembly-style production procedures, swept along the coast and around the world. The expansion of the commercial cannery fishery was not limited to France but was part of a worldwide development in which industrialism was incorporating peasant and tribal regions into a newly emerging global industrial-capitalist world system. Regions such as the Bigoudennie in which there were high levels of surplus labour and rural poverty were targeted by the canning firms.

The rapid transformation of the economy gave birth to a working class unfamiliar with the discipline that capital expected of its workers. The resulting militancy severely hindered the process of unfettered accumulation. While labour *power* may exist in the raw form, it must be made into a labour *force*. This requires coercing workers to accept conditions of labour dictated by the interests of capital as well as the workers' own accommodation and desire to change, adapt, and acclimatize to the new conditions.

The canners encountered two basic obstacles to their seemingly unstoppable expansion: an irregular supply of fish due to the seasonal nature of the fishery and a militant and politically radicalized workforce (Adam 1987; Chatain 1994, 40–43; Lachèvre 1994; Lebel 1981; Le Coz 1985; Martin 1994; Vauclare 1985; 1987). The supply of fish alternated between oversupply and scarcity and, given the demands of the organized working class, made ongoing profitability difficult. The canners responded to the militant labour movement by (1) requesting government-mandated control of supply; (2) introducing labour-saving technology to take over control of the work process; and (3) investing in fisheries in Portugal, Spain, Algeria, and Morocco.

Attempts were made to diversify into other fisheries (trap, longline, and tuna), but the success of this development was limited. The targeted species were not sufficiently profitable for the fish processors to encourage more than an occasional foray in new directions, though the tuna fishery did, to a certain extent, supply the canneries in times of undersupply or strike. Overall, however, the artisanal fishery was unable to supply the processing sector on a regular enough basis. Some canneries attempted to counteract the problem of irregular supply by switching to vegetables in the off-season, which in turn led to the development of back-breaking pea farming in the Penmarc'h peninsula. The canneries that survived into the 1960s were those that had turned away from fish processing and focused more generally on processing agricultural products.

In the 1950s the dominance of the sardine fishery began to wane under the pressure of competition from lower wage areas in the French colonial possessions (notably Algeria and Morocco) and Spain and Portugal. Without strong protective tariffs and/or greater rationalization, the local food-canning industry was non-competitive. Rationalization was not an option due to the strength of organized labour. Thus, by the early 1960s, most of the canneries had been shut down. In 2001, the two canneries remaining in the region primarily processed imported fish.

THE RISE OF THE TRAWL FISHERY

Between 1906 and 1945, the Bigouden fleet was completely transformed in terms of gear, vessels, and the structure of ownership. The cost of this transformation was underwritten by the Crédit Maritime, which was established by the French state in 1906, in part as a reaction to a crisis of undersupply in the sardine fishery and in part to assist artisanal fishers to purchase and outfit their own fishing vessels. Initially this worked to the interests of both canners and fishers. The canneries did not have to finance or own the fishing vessels, thus shifting the burden of economic risk. For the fishers, access to capital allowed them a modicum of independence from the canners, consistent with an artisanal mode of subsistence. It is important to point out that while the state was assisting fishers in becoming "little capitalists," it was significantly less supportive of other avenues of economic improvement, such as the formation of trade unions.

The primary technological transformation was the shift from sail to motor power and a gradual enlargement of the vessels themselves, partly to accommodate the added weight of the motors, and partly to take advantage of the vessels' newly extended fishing range and catching capacity. The first five motorized vessels were put into service in 1924. By 1934 the number had jumped to 634.

Ironically, the state-funded program of motorization figured prominently in the collapse of the sardine canners. The switch from sail to motor opened the door to the successful development of fisheries other than sardines and mackerel (the dominant fish species caught prior to the Second World War). During the war, ground fish (cod, sole, and other fish living on or near the ocean floor) became the most sought-after. This change in primary target was linked to the adoption of the trawl gear (a bag-shaped net dragged along the ocean floor to catch fish), made possible by the introduction of motorized vessels and hydraulics. By 1950, trawling was incontestably the primary focus of activity in the fishery. Whereas sardines were linked to the industrial canning plants in the region, the newly developed trawl fishery was oriented toward a fresh fish market based first in a regional network of small retailers and then in the large corporate distribution system of fish auctions and supermarkets.[3]

The introduction of trawl technology and the motorization of the fishing fleet cleared the way for the development of a relatively independent artisanal fishery to develop in the Bigoudennie. In the postwar period, trawling made it possible for the fishers to circumvent price and market controls by the canneries and to enter the rapidly growing fresh fish market, which was better suited to maintaining higher fish prices to fishers. Initially, fishers and fish buyers used the existing rail links to transport fish to market. Very quickly after the end of the Second World War, road and highway modernization programs made trucking more attractive due to its lower cost and greater flexibility.

The infrastructural support for the development of the sardine fishery was laid down by the railroad and the canning process. The postwar fishery developed in conjunction with the techniques of refrigeration and an expanding highway system that made it possible to ship fish by truck. The new reliance on truck transport—the major local trucking firm was established in Le Guilvinec in 1954—allowed a greater flexibility in marketing for fishboat owners. In the place of the departing canneries, a system of government-run fish auctions emerged. Fish auctions—*criées* in French—are now the primary mechanism for fishermen to sell their catch to potential buyers. Fish-processing firms (large and small) as well as fishmongers gather to participate in these daily auctions of fresh fish.

The shift away from an industrial cannery fishery to a fresh market artisanal fishery had a major impact on the structure of employment in the region. In this context, the fishery maintained a degree of economic independence. It is, however, a highly contingent independence because the industrial capitalist class is unwilling to take up the higher risk and lower rate of return involved in actually owning the boats. Moreover, the nature of fishing has its own allure, a gamble in which the chances of "winning big" loom large in the fishers' imagination—the more fish one can catch, the greater one's income. Yet it is unlikely that men could be enticed voluntarily to sea for wages. It is the possibility of the big pay-off that makes the brutally hard, physically taxing, and often poorly paid work bearable. The existence of an artisanal form of production throughout so much of the world's commercial fisheries can be seen only in this light.

While the employment of men on the fishboats remained relatively stable into the 1960s, employment prospects for women disappeared as the canneries

---

[3] The data for this observation derive from interviews with current (1995–96) fishers and archival sources located in the Departmental Archive, Quimper.

FIGURE 3.1: Fish buyers at the afternoon auction in Le Guilvinec

and subsidiary factories closed their doors and moved away. Ironically, at a time when the rest of rural Brittany was "modernizing," the Bigoudennie was experiencing a process of de-industrialization.

SOCIAL RELATIONS OF PRODUCTION

The basic conditions for an expanded and commercial fishery existed in the Bigoudennie for several decades before one could be launched effectively. As argued above, it was the railroad that made it technologically possible for the Bigoudennie to emerge as a fishing region and thus re-enter the national stage. However, the overall process of replacing human labour with machine labour in agriculture and the already existing (though small) fishery was predicated on wider social struggles occurring across France. In the Bigoudennie and in Brittany generally, the development of the industrial canning industry was marked by massive social struggles between the emergent working class and industrial capital. Specifically, Luddite protests fought machine technology. The successful introduction of industrial production was not pre-ordained. It required the complicity of the state (i.e., detailed police surveillance of workers and their organizations, suppression of strikes, and the support of management for labour-saving technologies) and the self-conscious organization of the capitalist class. We should note also that workers are not exploited by technology but by the social organization of production in which they are divorced from the products of their labour. This can be divided into three sites of labour: the household, the factory, and the fishery.

1. *The Household.* The point at which capitalist relations of production were inserted into the Bigoudennie was through kin relations within peasant households. This is not to say that wage labour was non-existent: it was a critical component of the agricultural economy. However, the dominant mode of expropriating surplus labour occurred within the medium of the family, where a gendered division of labour had a disproportionate effect on women and younger sons.

   According to Segalen (1991), these social relations of production were "egalitarian," and at points of generational succession "every one took their part." This view of the peasant relations of production overlooks certain critical aspects, discussed by Segalen herself. First, despite a system in which partible inheritance was the norm, the basic size of peasant holdings does not appear to have altered until the introduction of the commercial fishery, at which point they decreased in number while simultaneously increasing in size (Le Bail and Nicot 1995). This is partly accounted for by the form of landholding in the region in which peasants held short-term leases to farms and owned only the structures on the land. However, even though the splitting of a lease was possible, it appears that all effort was made to maintain economically stable farms through a commonly practised marriage pattern that served to maintain lease holdings of a viable size (Segalen 1991).

   Secondly, Segalen notes that population increases would have resulted in significant out-migrations throughout the late nineteenth and early twentieth centuries were it not for the arrival of the fishing industry. The "deus ex machina" of the fishing industry relieved the pressure on the peasant form of production by absorbing potentially surplus labour power. What Segalen does not discuss is the extent to which labour shunted into the fishery represented a "pushing" off the farm of those strategically disadvantaged in terms of control over the peasant means of production. In particular, women and younger sons lost their place on the farm and were either sent into the fishery in some capacity or had to leave the region.

2. *The Factory.* Social relations of production within the fish factories were unambiguously capitalist. The basic antagonism was that between owner/manager and worker. The social distance between them was exemplified in the differences between their housing. The owners and plant managers lived in large, château-like houses. They associated with the local notables

and middle classes in the local and regional capitals of Pont L'Abbé and Quimper. They spoke French and saw themselves as part of a national class. The workers were crammed into hovel-like houses (now prized as holiday cottages) with no sanitation or accessible sources of clean water. During the first 30 years of the sardine fishery, there were at least three cholera outbreaks in addition to rampant tuberculosis among the working poor.

Conditions of work left much to be desired, even by nineteenth-century standards. Employment was seasonal and job security was tenuous. The awful conditions of work and the callous disregard by owners and managers of workers' conditions were instrumental in the waves of strikes and protests that swept the region (see Chapter Two).

3. *The Fishery.* The struggle between boardroom calculations of profit and dockside desires to earn a living gave rise to a rather unique set of relations of production that are neither fully capitalist nor artisanal-based but locked through market circuits to capital and through labour requirements to family. This form of production resembles various types of "peasantries" or **simple commodity production.**

Several writers have effectively used the concept of simple commodity production to describe this form of production in the fishing industry (see, for example, Sinclair 1985), while others have attempted to argue that fisheries represent a full-fledged capitalist form of production as evidenced by the relationship between boat owner/skipper and crew (Clement 1986; Fairley 1985). The difference comes from whether one focuses on the kin-ordered aspect of resource pooling and labour recruitment or on the specific shipboard division of labour, allocation of surplus, and structure of ownership. Maddeningly, both perspectives are simultaneously correct and terribly wrong.

First, fisheries such as those in the Bigoudennie are fully formed "modern" artifacts created by industrial capitalism, not an archaic or pre-capitalist survival that has straggled along and fortuitously maintained itself despite all odds within an encompassing capitalist **mode of production.** The pattern is evident in just about every small- to medium-scale commercial fishery currently existing. It includes single vessel ownership, kin-based labour recruitment, super-exploitation of family labour power, full reliance upon the cash economy for all provisioning, and ties to a global or extensive regional capitalist commodity market. Sometimes previously existing "peasant" economies are incorporated within the fishery or these "peasant-like" economies may be created out of nothing (the British Columbia fishery is a case in point; see Menzies 1993). This is not to say there is no analytic value in using the conceptual framework of simple commodity production to understand this form of production. The danger is that in doing so one glosses over (perhaps even romanticizes) the pre- or anti-capitalist aspect of this form.

Second, the inherent problem of most of the "development of capitalism" theses is a teleological progression toward fully formed firms with clearly identifiable contradictory class relations, that is to say, the proletarian crewmembers against their bourgeois boat-owning skippers. The difficulty here is that in many cases the "natural" progression in commercial fisheries has been to move in the completely opposite direction. This is partly theoretical artifact and partly a misunderstanding of the actual nature of fisheries and an overemphasis on the harvesting side of the industry.

Let me explain: for much of the twentieth century, industrialized fisheries seemed to be pushing smaller-scale fishers out of business. Large vessels operating like seagoing factories appeared to be far more efficient than their smaller cousins. However, the high risk and level of capital investment required, combined with attempts by coastal nations to control adjoining ocean territory, have in most cases ultimately reduced the efficacy of large-scale fishing. By and large, it rapidly becomes more efficient for large firms to divest themselves of the harvesting end of fishing, shunting the risk onto individual boat owners. Long before notions of **flexible accumulation** and just-in-time production achieved notoriety as the dominant late-twentieth-century form of production, they had become the norm in fishing.

The strength of this particular set of relations of production structures and limits the possible adaptations of technology through the fishers' limited access to capital. But, importantly, the use of family labour (far easier to exploit than strangers) serves to depress the costs of production; hence, old technology is cheaper to employ and, ultimately, more productive than newer, potentially more efficient technologies.

Typically, it is only after the introduction of gear or licence limitations or through government-funded modernization programs that fishers begin to upgrade their gear and vessels. In Brittany, it was not until the Crédit Maritime began financing motorization that major change occurred. Then the change in propulsion systems opened the door to new fishing techniques, such as trawling. In hindsight, the introduction of motors and trawl gear foreshadowed the death of the local canning industry and made possible the survival of a family-based artisanal fishing industry.

CONCLUSION

The "episode of industrialization" in the Bigoudennie ended peasant agriculture in the region and laid out the foundation of the contemporary artisanal fishery. Despite the superficial similarities between the two, they are separated by the gulf of the industrial interlude. The contemporary fishing industry is a modern adaptation to the global market in fish products, government policy and subsidies, and the decline of fish stocks. In the following chapters, I turn away from the wider social processes of transformation and adaptation to consider the gendered worlds of work and work histories of individuals and their households in the contemporary Bigoudennie.

WORKING AT SEA

THE SOCIAL AND MATERIAL WORLD OF FISHERS is defined by their boats and the type of gear they use. Fishers often mark off the topography of their work and life histories by the names of the boats they fished on, the types of fish they caught, or the names of the men with whom they fished. I had many occasions as a child and adult working on the deck of fishboats in British Columbia to listen to genealogical listings of boats and crews as my father and his friends discussed and analyzed their world. Even today, my conversations with my father are often built around the names of fishers and their boats. In the Bigoudennie, despite the geographical and cultural distance from my hometown, naming boats and crews is also an important marker of social history.

As with many work worlds, the content of communication between fishermen in the Bigoudennie is centred around the **instruments of production**. Innovations and adaptations of gear and machinery—the tools for making a living—form the basis of many conversations. Fishers who are able to establish expertise in these areas and are able to convey this knowledge to others often find themselves at the centre of political movements as key knowledge holders and cultural brokers. This is so, I argue, because these fishers are able to mobilize others in their networks of information sharing, and, furthermore, the worth of their words has already been validated by their socially recognized expertise in the fishery.

In this chapter I describe the material work of fishing that, for the Bigouden fishers, is seen as the "real world": the world of fishing, boats, and gear. I am particularly interested in the structure of the working day, the nature of social class relations onboard the fishboat, the development of the Bigouden fleet, and the general characteristics of the boats themselves. This descriptive detail is important in understanding the lives of the fishers in the Bigoudennie. It is their experiences onboard the fishboats that defines them as fishers, and as such it is the background against which all of their political and social protests are enacted.

A DAY AT SEA

The 17-metre *Ann-Laura* is a typical local boat, a highly effective and modern all-weather steel dragger (trawler) built during the boom years of the 1980s. The covered work deck is cramped but keeps the crew protected from the rough seas typical of the open Atlantic. The wheelhouse sits amidships up above the work deck. The crew's quarters, engine room, and forward fish hold are located below decks. The galley, such as it is, is a small room just off the work deck. The wheelhouse is as well equipped as any that I have seen: it contains a GPS, loran, radar, depth sounder, sonar, and at least four or five radio phones.

The fishing day begins before daylight. On this trip, we left the dock at Le Guilvinec just after 3:30 a.m. It took about three hours to reach the fishing grounds 30 nautical miles offshore. When we arrived, there was a brief scurry of activity as the trawl was put in the water or "set." Then we waited. Not until the catch from the first drag is brought onboard two or three hours later does the work start in earnest.

The bag of fish is dumped out on the stern of the boat, the net is set back in the water, and then the crew sorts through the catch. The men get down on their hands and knees, moving quickly through the mound of langoustine and fish. Langoustine are sorted into two baskets according to their size; the fish are sorted by species. Close to 50 per cent of the catch is thrown back because it is either too small or not marketable. From the time this first load of fish comes on board until the fish is unloaded and sold, the work does not let up.

By 6:00 p.m. the fleet is back in port. The return of the fleet is a major attraction for tourists and residents alike. People start turning up at the harbour two hours early and transform the dock into a carnival-like atmosphere. Even on the coldest winter day, there can be as many as six busloads of tourists out to watch the unloading and auction.

Within minutes of landing against the quay, the skipper and crew are busy unloading their catch. The fish are sorted and placed into plastic boxes, which are brought onboard the boat. At dockside, these boxes are passed by hand off the boat and loaded onto carts, which are then wheeled directly

FIGURE 4.1 [*above*]: Cleaning and boxing langoustine for offloading on the way back to port; FIGURE 4.2 [*below*]: Repairing a tear in the trawl while at sea

onto the floor of the fish auction. The skipper checks that the fish have been properly sorted as his crew arranges the boxes on the auction floor. Almost as soon as they are done, the auctioneer arrives and begins the sale. From start to finish, the unloading process takes less than an hour.

I collected landing statistics from 15 fishboats representing the three general categories of vessels in the Le Guilvinec fleet and at three points in the annual cycle (February–March, June–July, and November–December). These periods correspond to changes in fishing patterns that are themselves the by-product of annual climatic conditions, availability of fish stocks, and market fluctuations. The skippers who supplied daily catch figures were recruited from among a core group of men whom I had first met on the bus trip to Nantes at the beginning of my fieldwork. While my sampling methods are at best haphazard, I had the advantage of being able to check the daily catch figures against the district-wide aggregate statistics collected by the regulating government agency, Affaires Maritimes, and the landing statistics reported in the local newspapers on a daily basis.

Data collected between 20 June and 23 July 1995 show that the *Ann-Laura* averaged a daily catch of 270 kilograms of fish for a landed value of 9,300 francs, approximately US$1,690. As this is a "live" fishery, most vessels in the *Ann-Laura*'s class (12–19 metres) return to port each afternoon to sell their fish. Daily gross crewshares are about 1,200 francs (US$218.00), nearly double the annual daily average of 660 francs (US$120.00) for fishers in the early 1990s. During the summer langoustine season, one of the more lucrative fishing seasons, the *Ann-Laura* fishes five days per week, 15 hours plus per day.

Between late September and early June (with the exception of the pre-Christmas season) the *Ann-Laura* makes trips of two to three days, landing in Le Guilvinec on Mondays, Wednesdays, and Fridays to take full advantage of both the auction schedule and available fishing time. During the winter season, the primary loss of fishing time is due to poor weather conditions. The worst time of the annual cycle is January–March, when low prices and bad weather combine to make earnings especially low.

On the *Ann-Laura* the net proceeds from the sale of fish is split 50/50 between the boat and crew. The division of the catch, or share agreement, between skipper and crew is fairly standard in the Bigoudennie. The only point of difference lies in the actual percentages accorded crew and skipper, which varies from between 30 and 70 per cent for the crew. The typical share division in the artisanal fleet is the same 50/50 split used by the skipper of the *Ann-Laura* (Chaussade and Corlay 1988). As an example, the division of the catch from the trip described above earned both the skipper and crew

TABLE 4.1

Typical average day's catch of a Bigouden dragger, 20 June to
23 July 1995

Gross sales	9,300 FF	US $1,690
Common charges[1]		
Landing taxes and charges (6% of gross)	558 FF	US $101
Fuel, lube oil, grease	900 FF	US $164
Social security charges[2]	833 FF	US $151
Food	112 FF	US $20
Net	6930 FF	US $1,254

[1] Costs incurred during the fishing process that are paid for by the boat owner include gear
  and equipment repairs.
[2] Social security charges are calculated on a fixed basis according to the certificate of each
  crewmember. In this case, the charges work out to about 9 per cent of the gross. These
  charges are commonly referred to as the "role." On some of the smaller boats, the role is
  paid for completely out of the boat share.

3,465 francs (US $1,254). Each of the four crewmembers received one-quarter
of the crew share, or 866.25 francs (US $157). As noted previously, the daily
earnings during this period are significantly higher than the previous year's
average daily earning, reflecting the higher earnings typical of the summer
months.

In 1995 the *Ann-Laura* was five years old. She had cost approximately 3.5
million francs to build. Payments are made on a quarterly basis. The loan
period is 15 years renegotiated every 5 years. The interest rate as of 1995 was
9.5 per cent, making the loan cost about 28,000 francs a year. Despite the
high cost of purchasing a fishing vessel—a steel dragger cost 3.1 million francs
in 1981, 4.8 million francs in 1985, and 6.4 million francs in 1992—Bigouden
fishing skippers have not hesitated in taking on sizeable loans in order to
purchase a vessel. The cost of carrying large boat loans is lightened somewhat
by a generous system of EU, state, regional, and departmental subsidies,
which in some cases can be as much as 45 per cent of the overall investment.
In 1990, for example, 11 new boats entered the fishery (seven boats of 18–25
metres, two of 16–18 metres, and two of 12–16 metres) worth a total of 62.2
million francs. The total subsidies represented 32.7 per cent of the investment
for the vessels in the 18–25-metre class, each of which cost approximately
4.5 million francs (Le Bail and Nicot 1995).

During the same period, a smaller dragger, the *Kervade*, had a gross sale of approximately 60 per cent of the *Ann-Laura*'s, that is, 5,500 francs. Even so, the average daily crewshare on the *Kervade* was roughly the same as on the *Ann-Laura* (860 francs versus 866.25 francs). The real difference is that the *Ann-Laura* can fish in much heavier seas than the *Kervade* and thus loses fewer days to bad weather. The *Kervade*'s financial manager, the skipper's wife, showed me a detailed graphical representation of the annual earnings; the months of January to March were almost at zero.

SKIPPERS, CREWS, AND THE FAMILY AT SEA

> We all work together, share the same risk: both physical and financial. The crew is like a second family. You spend 15 days at sea with your shipmates and two days at home. It's always a fight at home. You know your crew better than your family.
>
> —Union representative and former boat owner

What does it mean to compare one's work group with one's family but then to imply that the "real" family is beset by conflict? According to Michael Loti,[1] former skipper and district union representative on the local fishing committee, skippers and crews share a common interest: "We're all workers. The skipper-owner is every bit as much a worker as are his crewmembers." However, there are clearly identifiable social and economic distinctions between crews and skippers in terms of social networks and material assets. In this section, I examine the "family at sea," how it is constituted, in what sense we speak of social class on the fishboat, and in what ways the interests of skippers are parallel and/or antagonistic to those of their crews. My argument is that the social complexities of class onboard the Bigouden fishboat must be approached from two separate though intertwined positions. First, from the perspective of the family enterprise, we must consider how the structure of familial ownership shapes and/or constrains the social relations between crew and skipper through the reproduction of the fishing enterprise as a unit of production. Second, from the deck of the fishboat, we will see how the skipper's prerogatives are maintained and enforced on the boat and how the boat is organized as a site of production.

---

[1] Michael Loti is a pseudonym. I have chosen not to name the union as that would clearly reveal the identify of M. Loti.

In Part One, I discussed how fisherfolk in the Bigoudennie construct their self-image. The image is by no means homogenous, nor does it necessarily reflect the experiences of all those who live in the area. In Part Two, I examine the structure of their class relations, material conditions of life, and gendered processes of production. In this section, the pertinent questions are: How are boat-owning fishers to be conceptualized in class terms—as peasants, petty bourgeois, or disguised wage labourers? Where do their crews fit into the picture? Are crews unambiguously labour as viewed against skippers who are capital? How do ties of kin and community mediate or disrupt theoretical abstractions such as class?

Social class is, in this sense, more than just an objective relationship to the means of production: it must also be situated within the flow of time. It is my contention that a snapshot view of class obliterates the processes by which and through which individuals become members of social classes. In reverting to the ethnographic present, classes fade from view, leaving us with a field of social actors and a multitude of individual experiences. Abstracting social classes in this manner risks confusing stages in an individual's life history with actual class relations.

WORK FIRST! EAT LATER: SOCIAL CLASS AT SEA

The social relations on board a fishboat are typically governed by the necessity of the work process. The skipper runs the boat, chooses the fishing grounds, and gives the command to set and haul the net. The crew are responsible for the physical aspects of fishing, from setting the net to sorting the fish. The social space is implicitly divided into crew's space and skipper's space. This division is part functional (it would be next to impossible for the skipper to run the boat from the engine room) and part symbolic (several skippers actively discourage their crew from entering the wheelhouse unless they have been explicitly invited to enter). On one fishing trip, I witnessed a scene that, although not typical, clearly lays bare the social relations between crew as labour and skipper as capital.

The two deckhands had been busy sorting fish on their hands and knees for most of the morning. Occasionally, the skipper would walk back along the upper deck and yell down, "What's taking so long? There's nothing there!" Near noon, he came back and called out to one of the men, "It's time for lunch. Better put something on." The designated cook left the sorting and began to prepare a meal of boiled meat and chips for the skipper (the stove

FIGURE 4.3: On hands and knees sorting freshly caught fish

was too small to cook more than one meal at a time). When the meal was ready, he knocked on the wheelhouse door and handed it up to the skipper. He then started preparing a meal for the other crewmember and himself.

The skipper revved up the engine a notch, stuck his head down the companionway, looked around the galley, and told the cook to get ready to haul back the net. When the cook protested, the skipper simply reached across the stove and turned it off. Turning to the crewman he said, "Work first! Eat later."

This particular episode is singular in my observations in the Bigoudennie (though I have seen many such skippers onboard fishboats in British Columbia). Nonetheless, the actions of the skipper not only expressed his ultimate authority to command the labour of his crew but clarified the divergent social interests of crew and skipper. The skipper overlooks the time it takes for his crewmember to prepare his meal—in fact, he demands that time be taken. However, he does not tolerate the crewmember taking time to prepare food for himself and his mate—to do so is to take time away from the production of wealth for the skipper.

The social relations between crews and skippers are forged in a process of work that is both intimate and intense. Commercial fishers, especially on small- to medium-sized vessels, must constantly rely upon their workmates not just "to get the job done" but very often for their personal safety and well-being. The intensity of the emotions that arise can create enduring friendships and deeply felt animosities. In such a context, the social cleavages of class become obscured by the experience of having to personally rely on each other at points of crisis.

Crews who are unable to function in this manner do not stay together long. Yet there is a fundamental difference between the objectively defined interests of skipper-owners and crews. As owners of productive property, the skippers ultimately control the labour power of their crews irrespective as to whether the crews are family, friend, or strangers. However, in order to maintain their productive enterprises, the skipper-owners must also rely on the solidarity of their crews. As discussed in Part One, social solidarity has been maintained through an ideology of the local (Bigouden) and in the collective memory of past social protests (the Sardine Years). In this way, the divergent social interests of skippers and crews are erased in the cultural construction of a local identity.

Class is important, but, as I argue here, it has to be understood in a specific relationship to the messiness and situatedness of everyday life. Abstract models, appealing though they may be, can only be understood as guides to making sense out of social reality, not as social reality itself.

SOCIAL CLASS AND THE ARTISANAL FISHING ENTERPRISE

Much of the debate about class is merely an argument of classification, which is "in many cases a survey of the typology of class boundaries rather than a study of the process of class formation and the real historical battles which produce the ever-shifting lines of demarcation" (Stark 1980, 77). It is important to be cognizant of the "typologies of class boundaries" if only as a starting point in understanding the process that creates class. However, the explication of these typologies should not be an end in itself.

Admittedly, simple typologies of class boundaries typically employ a rigid structuralism that risks ignoring the contradictory and situational context of artisanal fishing communities such as Le Guilvinec. For example, Clement's notion of independent commodity producers (ICP)—those producers who are linked "with capital through the mechanism of the open market ... and are free of contractual obligations to capital" (1986, 64)—tends to ignore the common situation of occupational multiplicity among fishers, although this situation varies from fishery to fishery and, as in the case of the fishers in Le Guilvinec, is not always the rule.

Clement's framework includes a simultaneous consideration of social relations of production within the unit of production (i.e., the fishboat) and between units of capital (i.e., boats, processing firms, fish auctions, etc.); other typologies do not. The range of single-focus typologies stretches from the self-referential—"the fundamental division crosscutting all others is between those who think of themselves as labour and those who take on the self-image of owners, free enterprisers, or entrepreneurs" (Marchak 1984, 124)—to a structuralist materialism in which boat ownership is used as a measure to produce "a simple threefold categorization of class ... fishermen as owners; fishermen as rentiers; and crewmen ... who generally receive payment based on a predetermined share of the catch" (Guppy 1987, 19).

Other writers exclude the concept of class completely from their analysis of fishing peoples, adopting instead concepts such as network, action set, community, or adaptation. Acheson (1988), in his work on the lobster fishers of Maine, emphasizes networks and action sets as an adaptive mechanism in the face of uncertainty and risk. Anthony Cohen's work on the Shetland island of Whalsay is concerned with the symbolic construction of community "with its embeddedness in and influence on cultural and social relations." According to Cohen, "the fishing crew should be regarded as the community at sea" (1987, 145). John Forest inverts the relationship between social relations and ideological constructs and finds that "the decision to be a waterman [fisher] is itself founded on aesthetic desires" (1988, 105). Though these approaches to fishing do describe some aspect of the lived reality of fisherfolk, they ultimately fail in terms of providing an effective framework for understanding how such diverse groups of fishing people interact with the wider political economy within which they are embedded.

One way to situate fishers analytically is to isolate the enterprise of production (in our case, the family-owned fishing vessel) and to analyze it at two levels: "at the level of each enterprise [form of production] and at the level of the social totality of enterprises [mode of production]" (Banaji 1977, 9). Form of production "refers to the structure of the basic unit of production, as in, for example, the fishing crew" (Sinclair 1985, 15). This contrasts to the more comprehensive concept of the **mode of production** as "the dominant economic forces and relations of production in a society" (Sinclair 1985, 15).

Form of production "is conceived through a double specification of the unit of production and the social formation." By separating out these elements of fishers' lives, we can see both the structural similarities of their respective labour processes and the different historical developments and interactions between the fishers' units of production and the encapsulating capitalist mode of production. Thus, we can see how "the social formation provides the context for the reproduction of units of production [yet is] not uniquely determinative of the form of production" (Friedmann 1980, 160).

The identity of the form of production extant on the Bigouden fishboats is ambiguous and shifts depending on one's vantage point (i.e., from the basis of the shipboard crew or the household enterprise). These fishers can be understood by reference to either simple or capitalist commodity production. Simple commodity production "is a form of production which draws on the household for its labour supply and organizational structure; it depends on articulation with commodity markets to realize the value of what is produced and to acquire both personal and consumption goods and the means of production" (Sinclair 1985, 18). Furthermore, "in simple commodity production, the combined return to the enterprise and to labour generates no . . . tendency towards increased scale of individual enterprises" (Friedmann 1978, 88). On the other hand, capitalist commodity production "separates the direct producers from the means of realizing their labour and compels them into wage labour (or its equivalent, such as shares or piece-rates). Capital directly organizes production based on social labour, and the proletariat controls neither its product nor the labour process" (Clement 1986, 63).

Capitalist and simple commodity production are also distinguished by the form in which the reproduction of the enterprise occurs. The regeneration of the enterprise through time, from one cycle of production to the next, occurs in accordance with the logic of the form of production. In capitalist production "the appropriation of surplus value leads to accumulation within the enterprise; this generates an inherent tendency toward concentration or increased scale of production independent of technological advances" (Friedmann 1978, 88). Excepting, for the moment, changes in the scale of production resulting from technological innovations, "there are no economic pressures in simple commodity production for expanded reproduction; that is, simple reproduction, or maintenance of production at the existing level, is adequate for survival of each unit of production"; simple commodity production is, however, subject to "demographic pressures which lead enterprises with more than one son to seek expanded reproduction" (87).

The process of expanded reproduction differs depending on the form of production. Under a capitalist form of production, expanded reproduction tends toward concentration and accumulation. In simple commodity production, expanded reproduction tends "toward fission, in which income generated in one household enterprise is used to establish a new one on the same scale" (Friedmann 1978, 88). Thus, expanded reproduction within a simple commodity form of production will increase competition between units of production whereas it decreases such competition under a capitalist form of production. This is especially important in open access fisheries.

The notion of capitalist commodity production allows us to identify a set of antagonistic social classes (capital/labour or, in this case, skipper/crew). The concept of simple commodity production identifies "a class of combined labourers and property owners within a capitalist economy ... the circuits of reproduction of simple commodity production intersect with those of commodity, landowning, and banking capital, and with markets in labour power, in abstractly determined relations" (Friedmann 1980, 162). The analytic task is to link abstractions, such as class typologies, with lived experience but without recourse to a naïve empiricism in which the uniqueness of the group of fishers is overemphasized.

In the story I told above, the skipper was clearly attempting to demonstrate and enforce his authority. Here the lines between boss and worker were clearly drawn. But there is also that other image, the image of the family as invoked by men like Michael Loti when they talk about the family-like relationship between skippers and crew and why they belong in the same union. Both images are right, yet both are also only partial. This is the ambiguity of a form of production that relies upon kinship and friendship-like relationships—ultimately as idioms of community—to ensure the reproduction of family-based enterprises within a capitalist economy.

THE DEVELOPMENT OF THE BIGOUDEN FISHING FLEET

Two major waves of innovation and technological development played a role in the development of the contemporary Bigouden fishing fleet. First, the switch from sail to motor was instrumental in changes in gear type (from drift nets to seine and trawl) and in target species (from sardines to bottom fish). The second major change involved new materials such as steel and aluminum and innovations in trawling techniques, primarily from side to stern trawling.

The switch from sail to motor propulsion created the technical capacity for an artisanal trawl fishery. Compared to steam-powered vessels, internal combustion engines are cheaper, smaller, and therefore more readily adaptable to family-based enterprises. Motor-powered vessels also afford greater control and manoeuvrability, which in turn result in increased access to fishing grounds during periods of windless days and inclement conditions that would have kept sailing vessels in port. Motors also expand the effective range of the fishboat, bringing fishing grounds farther afield within reach.

They also make it possible to fish in deeper water than before (an important factor for catching bottom fish) and thus have brought new species of fish within reach of exploitation. All together, motorization has provided the technological basis for the expansion of family-owned artisanal fishboats.

The first steel-hulled trawler used in the artisanal fishery was a 22-metre vessel built in 1963 at Dunkirk, but widespread use of steel-hulled vessels in the northern French artisanal fishery did not occur until 1968. Nevertheless, stern trawling began to appear in the artisanal fishery nearly ten years after its introduction in the industrial-class fishery (vessels greater than 25 metres). The switch to stern trawling was made possible by the installation of gantries on the stern of the vessel and the addition of a fixed stern ramp. Working conditions were improved by the addition of a covered or semi-covered deck on which the wheelhouse was perched amidships (Dorval 1987). According to Dorval, "there was some resistance at that time (1970–72) among Breton fishermen to vessels with covered decks and stern trawling facilities" (1987, 26). The first steel-hulled and covered deck vessel in Brittany entered the fleet in 1972. Within ten years, it was the preferred vessel type for new construction (see Table 4.2).

The general layout of contemporary vessels emerged in the 1970s. The basic features are sleeping quarters for the crew in the stern with a separate stateroom for the skipper on the larger vessels, engine in the middle, and the fish hold in the forward section. Hydraulic winches appeared in 1970–71 and net drums in 1972. Initially, the vessels were equipped with only one drum; today, most have two or three. The drums are used for storage and hauling of the nets.

There are four main jobs aboard the Bigouden draggers: skipper, deckboss, engineer, and deckhand. With the exception of the larger-class vessels (20–24 metres), there is no designated cook's position. Crewmembers often perform more than one task.

The work pattern can be broken into six primary stages: setting and hauling the net, sorting and storing the catch, miscellaneous tasks, meals, rest periods, and watches on the bridge. The actual setting and hauling of the net takes very little time. However, this is also the most dangerous and difficult of the fishing operations and the point when the greatest number of accidents occur. Sorting the catch is backbreaking work, often done on one's hands and knees with the deck shifting and rolling underfoot. On smaller vessels the skipper may put the boat on auto-pilot and come down to the work deck and assist with sorting the catch.

Day boats are usually out of port for about 14 hours each trip. This often entails leaving and returning in the dark. They are thus restricted in terms

TABLE 4.2

Changes in the construction of 19 to 26-metre trawlers: Wood versus steel, 1956–83

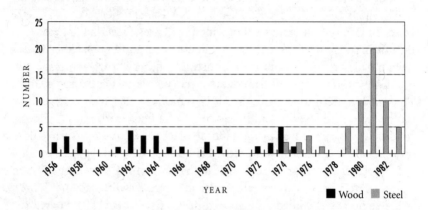

of their fishing grounds, having to fish within a three- or four-hour travelling radius of port so that they are able to arrive in time for the Monday to Friday afternoon auctions. A typical day trip involves setting and hauling the drag three or four times, leaving the crew little time to rest between sorting the catch and preparing to set and haul the nets.

On vessels making trips of between three and 14 days, the fishing process continues almost without interruption. The crew, skipper, and mate work in shifts, grabbing rests in between tows and after the fish have been sorted and stored in the fish hold. While crew and skipper usually have between eight and ten hours of rest in every 24, they rarely have more than four hours of uninterrupted sleep (Dorval 1987).

In his study of working conditions and security at sea in the early 1980s, Dorval notes that the typical crew size varies between five and eight (1987, 196). One of the direct impacts of the crisis of the early 1990s was a reduction in average crew sizes to between three and six men. The average crew size in the near-shore fleet is effectively three men on board the vessel at any one time. The offshore vessels (20–24 metres) have reduced their crew to between five and six men, with one crewmember taking a trip off every four or five trips. The reduction of crew, while helping to maintain the fishers' incomes, has had an immediate and deleterious effect on the conditions of work. Anecdotal evidence collected from fishing skippers and local fishing companies suggests that reduced crew sizes are workable but do result in increased injuries at sea.

BOATS AND THEIR GENERAL CHARACTERISTICS

The contemporary Bigouden fishing fleet is composed primarily of steel-hulled vessels of between 12 and 24 metres in length. The group of under 12-metre vessels represents a very different form of fishery from the larger class. The smaller boats tend to be older, fishing just off the adjoining coast, and their operators tend to engage in a multitude of subsistence practices. The operators and deckhands on the larger vessels, on the other hand, are more likely to be full-time fishers.

The majority of vessels in the contemporary fleet (301, representing practically all of the 12–24-metre vessels) are engaged in bottom or mid-water trawling. A funnel-shaped net, held open by two large "doors," is towed along the bottom from the stern of the fishboat. The net scoops up practically everything in front of it. It is hauled up onto the vessel every two or three hours, the catch is loaded on board, and then it is set out again. Four other gear types are commonly used: gill and/or trammel netting (9 boats), long-lining (10 boats), trap fishing (15 boats), and seining for sardines (6 boats).

TABLE 4.3
Bigouden fishing fleet by length, power, and tonnage, 1995

Length	Number	Power (kW)*	Tonnage*
>12 m	169	11,122	939
12–16 m	135	27,451	4,014
16–25 m	156	53,297	9,277
25–38 m	1	348	107
Total	461	92,218	14,337

* Figures represent the combined power/tonnage of all boats in each length category.

TABLE 4.4
Bigouden fishing fleet by length and age, 2000

Length	<10 yrs	10–15	15–20	20–25	>25 yrs	Total
<12 m	6	26	26	39	72	169
12–16 m	12	17	18	26	62	135
16–25 m	28	41	53	15	19	156
>25 m					1	1
Total	46	84	97	80	154	461

The effective maximum age of a fishing vessel in the district is 20 years. There is a significant age discrepancy between the 169 vessels in the under 12-metre class and the 12–24-metre class. The vast majority of the smaller class is older than 20 years, while the average age of close to 75 per cent of the larger class is younger. This discrepancy reflects differential funding opportunities for the building of larger vessels during the late 1970s and 1980s. As part of the modernization plans of the postwar era, plus fleet de-commissioning schemes, vessels older than 20 years in the 16-metre class can be destroyed and the owner compensated for removing the boat from the fleet. The net effect has been a growth in larger, more efficient vessels and a progressive aging of the smaller boats.

CONCLUSION

Fishing is one of the most dangerous and difficult occupations in the world. This is so even when one considers the many improvements over the past century in working conditions on board boats such as those in the Bigouden fleet. Early boats were completely reliant on the fickleness of weather and the skills of their crews. Navigation was done without any of the aids that today's fishers take for granted. However, even with these real improvements, fishers still live very much at the mercy of the sea. The tempo of work, though mediated by modern improvements, is still set by the whims of tides, winds, and ocean storms. During the fall of 2000, for example, three Breton fishing boats and ten men were lost at sea while fishing.

The physicality of the work, the necessity of relying on one's workmates, and the strong sense of uncertainty in what one's catch will be underlie the fisherman's near obsession with his boat and its gear. The brief account given in this chapter of a day spent at sea offers a glimpse into the setting in which fishers work. The discussion of changes to gear and fishboats plus the general description of the characteristics of the boats and the jobs involved in the fishing process are important factors that help make sense of the fishers' world. They are, however, only one small part of the fishing community. As discussed in the following chapter, the work that artisanal fishermen do is made possible by the work that women do ashore.

WORKING ASHORE

THE MOST OBVIOUS PUBLIC EXPRESSION of the boundary between men and women can be found in the gatherings of women, young children in hand, waiting dockside for their men to return from the sea. I cannot help but read into this scene my own memories. My childhood involved what felt like long hours of waiting for a late-night phone call from my father. My mother would telephone the other wives and girlfriends to tell them that the boat would soon be back. We never knew the precise time of arrival—there was always an error factor of a couple of hours one way or another. But once the call came in, everything stopped. Off we would go to wait at the dock for the first sign of his boat rounding the breakwater. As I, the anthropologist, stand waiting on this Breton dock, slightly to the side and behind the gathered crowd, I see my own eagerness at my father's arrival reflected in the faces of the restless waiting children. Summoned by the skipper's wife, as my mother had called her friends years earlier, the children and their mothers were waiting to celebrate the boat's return.

When I ask about the difficulties of being a fisherman's wife, about how one arranges daily life to this non-terrestrial rhythm, the waiting women respond in a rather matter-of-fact way: "It's just the way things are. This is what it is to be a fisherman's wife." Revealed in their dockside conversations is neither fear nor worry. This is neither the time nor the place for anxiety. In their homes, however, several of the women open their books and show me, in graphs and tables of past income, the yearly variations of catch, price, weather, and mechanical breakdowns. It is as if, in the simple act of graphing and drawing it out on paper, the unknowns of living as a fisherman's wife can be conquered and taken into account.

What I witness on the dock is the most visible manifestation of gender roles. In one sense, this scene presents and reinforces a particularly "traditional" image of men and women in fishing (and, one might add, in Western society in general). This is especially so because it is wrapped in metaphors of family and images of children. Very clearly the homecoming of one's partner, father, or son is a powerful public manifestation of gendered social relations (among other things). It is not, however, the full picture.

In this chapter, I examine the specific ways in which relations of production and consumption in the Bigoudennie are structured by notions of gender. I do this by reference both to the gendered division of labour with respect to waged labour and non-waged labour critical to household maintenance and reproduction and to the manner by which differences in a household's economic enterprise are reflected in women's experience of work.

FISHERMEN AND WOMEN IN FISHING COMMUNITIES: A GLOBAL OVERVIEW

The worlds of women and men are perhaps nowhere more separated than in commercial fishing communities. Beyond the very real physical and spatial separation in which men are away at sea and women stay ashore is a symbolic structure that is at once affirmative of the role played by each gender and retrogressive in its inherent segregation. Work and home, men and women— this most hackneyed bipolarity echoes through time in different versions, the most common of which is the nature/culture model (for a nuanced discussion, see Ortner 1974). The literature on the sexual division of labour is replete with examples of occupations, tasks, or behaviours defined as "masculine" in one culture but "feminine" in another (Mead 1935). Fishing remains, however, awkwardly positioned in the academic literature as a decidedly masculine pursuit across cultures as diverse as Aboriginal North Pacific America, South Asia, West Africa, and coastal Europe.

To unearth examples of women's involvement in fisheries, one must either expand the definition of fishing to include such tasks as fiscal management of the fishing enterprise, fish processing, and marketing of the fish or lump together all manner of different subsistence practices that include some aspect of the capture of fish. Each of these paths has expanded our understanding of "fishing" and is important *vis-à-vis* equity politics: they remind us that there is no "natural" reason to exclude women from actively engaging as "fishermen." Important symbolic/cultural explanations for the exclusion

of women from fishing all centre on notions of patriarchy and the maintenance of male privilege. Male working-class notions of self, for example, are
intimately tied up in demonstrating that one is *not a woman*. In a discussion
of British Columbia halibut fishers, I delved into the symbolic importance
(in terms of male gender ideology) of defining the fishery as an exclusively
male domain (Menzies 1991). Contemporary academic politics notwith-
standing, the capture of fish and the crewing of boats is definitionally male
in the Bigoudennie and most other places in our world.

Estimates of female participation, based on work in the American Pacific
Northwest (Allison, Jacobs, and Porter 1989), British Columbia (Jensen 1995),
and Alaska (Fields 1997), suggest that between 5 and 10 per cent (or less) of
the fishers are female. In 1994–95 in the maritime administrative district of
Le Guilvinec, only 6 out of more than 1,600 registered fishers were women.
In 2010 this number had dropped to three. One woman owned her own 6-
metre vessel; the other women fished either with their husbands or some
other male relative. None of the women fished on deep-sea vessels in the
24-metre class. Irrespective of the multitude of potential causal explanations,
the continuation of a system of rigid gender separation underlies a particularly
masculine conception of identity based on the denial of physical discomfort
and an intense "physicality." Fishers work under difficult and dangerous conditions. They experience chronic back pain, persistent soft-tissue arthritis,
and carpal tunnel syndrome caused by repetitive motion. Yet ask a fisher if
he has sustained a serious injury and the most likely answer, despite any
physical evidence to the contrary, may well be, as Marion Binkley (1995) dis-
covered, "no."

In a study on risk and danger in the Nova Scotia offshore fishery, Binkley
encountered fishers with visible injuries, such as amputated fingers. When
she asked if they had had a serious injury while at sea, they said "no." When
pressed to explain a lost finger, for example, the reply was, "'You know, you
stop fishing after you have a serious accident.' Since those men could still
fish, they felt they had never had a serious accident" (Binkley 1995, 138–
39). Binkley correctly identifies this denial (and glorification) of mutilation
and of working through pain and fatigue as part of a masculinist ideology, an ideology that simultaneously keeps men working under ghastly
conditions and provides them with an explanatory system that justifies
their actions, even to the extent of making a virtue out of it (see also Walker
1988).

In many fisheries worldwide, the men are away from their home communities for long periods of time. Depending upon gear type (net, line, or

trap), species fished (ground fish, herring, tuna, etc.), or the regulatory regime under which fishing occurs, they may be away from their homes for 250 to 300 (or more!) days of the year. The overall effect of this is women-centred[1] families in which women take on the primary role of the maintenance and day-to-day management of the household in a manner akin to a single-parent household.

Women play an integral role in most fisheries. Their location at home places them in the centre of the political and economic fields within which it has become increasingly important to act. As the market for fish products has been globalized and local protective tariffs removed (in the EU, primary tariff barriers for fish products were removed in 1993; see Arbo and Hersoug 1997), the political role played by women in the home community has expanded to take on a wider national and international dimension (Clark 1988; Smith 1988). In addition to their expanding political role, women are the primary caregivers for children and maintain and provision the home. Skippers' wives often manage the fishing boat's accounts. Over and above all of this, many fishermen's wives are also employed in wage labour outside the home.

WOMEN'S WORK AND FISHING IN THE BIGOUDENNIE: "WITH ONE HAND I FEED MY FAMILY, WITH THE OTHER I FIGHT FOR OUR SURVIVAL"

Bigouden women from fishing families play a crucial role in the economic, social, and cultural survival of their families and households. Pascale Le Guin, whose words to me are used in the title to this section, clearly articulates how being politically active is tied to the economic viability of her family. Like all women from fishing families, she is very aware that her paid and unpaid labour is critically important in the household economy. This section describes the general structure of women's work and then explores the specific differences of women's experiences in terms of the scale of their respective household enterprises.

Much of a woman's unpaid labour in the Bigoudennie is determined by

---

[1] In her study of maritime households and the women at the centres of them, Sally Cole suggests using the term "women-centred" over such terms as matricentric or matrifocal— terms that "tend to emphasize the centrality of the mother in household relations, whereas, 'women-centred' acknowledges the centrality of women in general, regardless of kinship" (1991, 62). I have, accordingly, adopted the term.

whether or not she has children. The existence of a well-funded (by North American standards) crèche and pre-school system releases, to a certain ex- tent, parental labour (predominantly female) for waged labour in other sec- tors of the economy. Nonetheless, the "family" is the primary site of domestic labour, and in the Bigoudennie it is predominantly the domain of women. The issue of the family as the site both of the reproduction of labour power and of the oppression of women has been much debated. Two particularly good discussions of these issues, if somewhat dated, can be found in Michèle Barrett (1980, see especially 152–226) and Lise Vogel (1983, see especially 136– 75). Women's tasks in the domestic sphere can be broken into three basic categories: (1) children, (2) housekeeping, and (3) financial management.

1. *Child care* is partially underwritten by the state in the form of an extensive pre-school system. In Brittany, nearly 80 per cent of children aged two and up are in the school system, and more than 95 per cent of three-year- olds attend school. (I appreciated the benefits of the French school system for my two sons and still marvel that people we met early in our stay, upon learning we had two young boys, asked when, not if, we would be enrolling them in school.)

   The benefits of a state-funded child-care system are not to be under- estimated. However, the primary responsibility for children in the fishing community (and in general) falls to women. The specific impact of having children varies according to the mother's age and degree of self-reliance. Children add to the burden of household labour for quite a few years before they can usefully be seen as net contributors to the household (in terms of labour devoted to the household versus labour created for others).[2]

2. *Household tasks* include cleaning, maintenance, shopping, cooking, and laundry, just to name the most obvious. Housework is a particularly vexing vocation: the more accomplished one becomes, the less obvious one's labour appears. It is far more apparent when a house is untidy than when it is neat and orderly.

---

[2] As a father who has been intimately involved in my children's lives, I recognize the strong emotional and affective ties parents develop with their children and appreciate that it is a potentially "insensitive" evaluation of the impact of children to focus on their material impacts on household labour as opposed to other factors. Yet I am also enough of a mate- rialist to realize, as a parent in contemporary society, that my unpaid labour in the home subsidizes the reproduction of capitalism in a fundamentally important way that should not be overlooked.

3. The majority of the *financial work* in the home is also conducted by women. This includes keeping the household accounts (the fishing accounts too, if the woman is married to a skipper) and ensuring that regular household bills are paid. As almost anyone who has tried to balance a budget and provision a household will attest, the job of household finance is a delicate balance between controlling family desires and meeting basic needs. This job extends into the planning of daily, weekly, or monthly shopping trips. With children in the house, ensuring appropriate clothes, toys, and supplies can be a daunting task, especially if one's income is declining or insufficient to meet basic needs. Working outside the home further complicates one's tasks on a given day.

To further contextualize this daily round, I describe below the typical work patterns of three women: Jeanne Floch (whose husband skippers an 18-metre steel dragger), Marie Le Roche (whose husband skippers a 12-metre wooden dragger), and Pascale Le Guin (whose husband is a deckhand on an 18-metre steel dragger). Drawing from interviews and observations in the mid-1990s, these stories reflect typical households involved in the Bigouden fisheries.[3]

JEANNE FLOCH

Jeanne's husband, Étienne, is a fishing skipper who owns an 18-metre steel dragger and whose fishing trips range from one to four days in length with a crew of four, including himself. They have three school-aged children—Jannick, 8; Yves, 6; and Matthew, 5—and live in a rather spacious home built in 1987 and just inland from Le Guilvinec in the commune of Plomeur.

Jeanne's primary responsibility is the basic accounting and record keeping of the fishing enterprise. She keeps track of the boat's tally slips and receipts for trip expenses. Though it is her husband who actually "makes" most of the purchases, she is the one who records them and maintains the records. She meets on a regular basis with a business representative of the local management co-operative who does the family-fishing enterprise's detailed fiscal planning.

Jeanne is also responsible for relaying messages between the boat and the crewmembers' wives and partners when the boat is at sea for more than a day at a time. Given the regularity of the boat's schedule, this is normally

---

[3] The stories of these three women come from conversations and interviews conducted from October 1994 to November 1995 and on subsequent visits between 1998 and 2008.

not a particularly taxing responsibility. However, in the event of an accident at sea, the task of calling the affected wife falls to Jeanne.

Jeanne does not currently work outside the home, although she has worked in the past as a retail clerk. She resigned her previous job before the birth of her first child. At several points in our conversation, she discussed the possibility of returning to work, especially given the downturn in the fishing economy. In light of the crisis, however, she felt it was unlikely that she would find a job since many other women were looking for employment in spite of the overall decline in employment in the region. Between her responsibilities for the fishing enterprise and her children, she said, she was better off at home. "As long as Étienne is fishing, we seem to be all right. He is very good at catching fish. When the crisis hit, we were in a good position. We hadn't over-extended like some of the others who are worse off did. It's much harder for others than for us." Jeanne's work in the home includes basic household cleaning, laundry, cooking, purchasing food and clothes, and looking after the children.

Jeanne's daily schedule is shaped by the rhythm of her children's schooling. School starts at 8:50 a.m., breaks from 11:50 to 2:00 for lunch, and is finished at 5:00 p.m. Most days she picks her children up and drives them home for lunch, but she also participates in an informal lunch co-op with three or four other mothers. When she is unable to take her own children home for lunch, one of the other mothers will take them. The children could stay at school and have lunch at the cafeteria, but Jeanne prefers that they have a home lunch.

On a typical day, Jeanne will prepare about six separate meals. When her husband is fishing day trips out of Le Guilvinec, the evening before he sails she makes a small bag lunch and breakfast for him to take on the boat. In the morning, she prepares a light breakfast for the children and herself before school. She eats lunch with the children during the noon break and prepares a light meal for them when they come home from school. And she has supper waiting for her husband when he comes home from the boat in the early evening after unloading the day's catch.

For most of her day-to-day shopping (bread and dairy supplies), Jeanne drives to the nearby town of Plomeur. On Saturdays the whole family (including her husband when he is in town) goes to Pont L'Abbé to shop for the week's groceries at a large supermarket. Occasionally they will make a special trip into Quimper, 40 kilometres away. On Thursdays, after dropping her children off at school, Jeanne goes to the open-air market in Pont L'Abbé.

All in all, Jeanne's daily labour in the home provides an important material contribution to the economic and social well-being of her household. Despite her being fairly well-off in local terms, the cost of replacing her labour would be crippling to the family budget. The value of "domestic" labour has been well documented (see, among others, Benston 1969; Secombe 1974; Beechey 1977). In Jeanne's case, her unpaid labour frees capital from the family fishing enterprise so that it can be reinvested in maintaining their productive property (i.e., boat and gear).

MARIE LE ROCHE

Marie's husband, Jean, skippers a 12-metre wooden inshore dragger with a crew of two, including himself. They have two teenage children—Anna, 17, and Jean-Pierre, 15. The crisis of the early 1990s caught the Le Roches in the process of renovating their old farmhouse near Lesconil, work that is now deferred until the fishery recovers. They had resisted investing in a larger, modern steel dragger during the 1980s boom, opting instead for a more conservative fiscal path. Nonetheless, the impact of collapsing fish prices forced them into a process of "retrenchment" and effecting "budgetary efficiencies" (to borrow from the neo-liberal vocabulary of contemporary budget cutting).

The rhythm of school has less of an impact on Marie's daily activities than on Jeanne's. Marie's children attend the lycée (high school) in Pont L'Abbé. They leave by bus every morning before 8:00 a.m. and return home by 6:00 p.m. "My time is a little more my own now that the children are adolescents. When they were little, they took a lot of time out of my day," Marie says. She also expects them to shoulder some of the basic household tasks including cooking, some shopping, and light housecleaning.

"I'm still the boss here," she tells me, laughing. As if to demonstrate, she calls out to her daughter, "Anna, let's have some coffee for our guest." Turning to me, she adds, "She doesn't make very good coffee. I'll be right back." While waiting for her to return, I sit back and look around the dining room. I've been sitting here for nearly an hour listening to her talk about fishing, the crisis, and her day-to-day work in the home and for the family-fishing enterprise. The room is large enough to hold a table that must seat at least 25 people. It is made from a richly textured hard wood and is ornately decorated. Heavy, dark brown buffets and china cabinets (typically "Breton" and decidedly not "nouveau") are arranged along three sides of the room, which serves as a combination office, parlour, and formal dining room (the family eats meals around a small table in the kitchen). A wide bay window faces the street; it's part of the recent spate of renovations, I suspect. My reverie is broken by the arrival of two family friends. Marie introduces me, saying,

"He wants to know about the crisis." Anna brings in the coffee, and Marie returns to telling me about her daily work as a fisherman's wife.

Marie is far more involved in her family's fishing enterprise than is Jeanne. "The more things I do," she said, "the more money we have. For example, I buy the provisions for the boat. On the bigger boats, they get a supply company to buy it for them. But that costs more." She stands up and takes a notebook from a nearby cabinet in which she keeps the fishing records. She passes the notebook to me. I see that it is really a calendar, one month per two pages. A sequence of dates is marked off in a variety of colours.

"Here, these dates—that's when the boat loan must be paid. It's a priority, red ink."

"These ones," she points to days marked in blue, "that's the gear account at the Co-op. Important, but we can let it slide a little."

"Over there, in green, that's when the fuel account must be paid."

She returns to the cabinet, looks through a shelf of notebooks, and pushes another one across the table to me. "This shows our gross earnings over the past five years by fishing day and month."

Every contingency is detailed and graphed: days lost due to bad weather or mechanical breakdowns, cycles in fish prices (mostly downward over the past several years, I note), and gross stock and overall expenditures.

"I do all this," she says. "This way I know exactly what is happening. I can plan household expenditures. Here, look at this," she points to a low point on the graph. "That's late January, early February. The weather is so bad he can't get out of the harbour some days. So, I know I have to save up a little, put some aside. It's not easy."

Marie also works outside of the home. She has a paper route of 150 deliveries spread across a rural area of close to 150 square kilometres. "I get up at the same time as Jean leaves to go fishing. It takes me about three or four hours from the time I pick up the papers till I'm back home." Marie applies the money she earns from the paper route against the household food budget—"that's one less thing to worry about," she says.

PASCALE LE GUIN

Pascale's husband Henri is currently a deckhand on a three-man wooden dragger fishing out of Lesconil. According to Pascale, the boat seems to always be *en panne*, or broken down. "First it's the hydraulics, then they rip up the net, next it's the engine. Henri's got to find a better post." Pascale and Henri have two children—Sophia, 7, and Jannick, 5. They live in a small rented home in Loctudy. "We need a nicer place for the children," says Pascale, "but with the fishing the way it is, there is no certainty. Henri will have to get on a better boat. Maybe one of the Bara boats."

The Bara boats are a small fleet of 24-metre steel draggers owned by a local boat-owning company based in Le Guilvinec, Armament Bigouden. Each boat's name begins with the word *bara,* which means bread in the Breton language. This fishing enterprise is notable because it is one of only two family businesses that own more than two or three boats. Also, while other enterprises are either standing still or going backward, the Armament Bigouden has been able to expand its fleet.

As the wife of a deckhand, Pascale has no responsibilities directly related to the fishing process (though she does make a bag lunch for Henri to take with him on the boat). She is employed part-time as a cleaner in a nearby health-care facility. The crisis hit their household hard. Her husband's income dropped by nearly 40 per cent at the peak of the crisis. "We were planning to have a house built just when the prices started to fall. It was too much, so here we are," Pascale says. In 1995, Henri's fishing income increased slightly but was still close to 20 per cent lower than its 1992 level. "While our income goes down, everything else goes up."

Pascale's response to the crisis is both pragmatic and political. In the first instance, she has taken on a number of private housecleaning and domestic jobs. On the political level, she has joined the Fishermen's Wives Committee. "With one hand I feed my family," she says, "with the other I fight for our survival."

When she works, Pascale's children stay in school over lunch. "I'd like to take them home for lunch, but I have to work. They get a good meal. It's good for them to start early. Education is what will give them their jobs. They can't count on fishing, especially since they are girls."

Arranging her schedule is one of the most difficult aspects of Pascale's day. As a part-time worker she does not have a regular schedule and so must constantly juggle her commitments to her children and work. She relies upon her retired mother to help out. In return, Pascal helps her mother maintain her home, does odd jobs for her such as shopping, and supplies her with fish whenever she can from Henri's share of take-home (this amounts to about once a week at least). Pascale definitely does not see this as an exchange: "it's what any daughter would do."

Although both Pascale and Henri come from families with four or more generations in the fishery, neither one believes their daughters will marry a fisherman or stay in the area as adults. As essentially propertyless workers, they have very little to pass on to their children that would keep them in the region. They look toward the institutions of the contemporary welfare state to provide their girls with a "good job."

SOCIO-ECONOMIC DIFFERENCES AND WOMEN'S WORK

Jeanne Floch, Marie Le Roche, and Pascale Le Guin share a common local experience as fishermen's wives. However, their social worlds and their material conditions are quite different. Most obvious is the difference between Pascale, whose husband is a deckhand, and the lives of the other two women whose husbands own fishing boats. Pascale's economic well-being is far more contingent and unstable than either of the other two. Neither she nor her husband came from families who owned land or any other form of productive property.

Despite the fact that both Jeanne's and Marie's households own productive property (i.e., a fishboat), their economic opportunities are not the same. Here it is the scale of their household's fishing enterprise that makes the difference. For Jeanne, her family's relatively large and more economically productive fishboat results in a correspondingly larger household income. The crisis of the mid-1990s did affect their fishing enterprise but nowhere near as severely as it did households of deckhands or those boat-owning families who owned smaller, less efficient vessels. For households like Marie's, the crisis was particularly difficult. Given their investment in a fishing boat, they were not able to leave the region in search of work without trying either to lease out their boat or to sell it at a price that would preserve their investment, so they stayed in the region. The crisis also made it harder to keep crewmembers who either left for work on more productive vessels or left the region in search of better employment.

Unlike Jeanne, Marie and her husband did not have as large a financial cushion to fall back on. The more productive boats were able to make do by reducing their crew size from five to four, cutting back on the replacement and maintenance of old gear, and increasing their fishing effort. Smaller boats were already at the limit of this sort of economizing and thus had next to no financial reserves. Of those experiencing the crisis, it was this category of household enterprise that was most in danger of defaulting on their loans and going bankrupt.

Having successfully weathered the crisis of the 1990s, Marie says, "from the vantage point of 2000 I don't know how we did it. Henri and I made a lot of sacrifices, but it feels like a miracle that we still have our boat and our house. So many others lost everything." Emergency government plans introduced in 1995 and 1996, combined with modest increases in the price for fish, managed to ameliorate the crisis to a certain extent. However, during the crisis itself nearly 25 per cent of vessels between 11 and 24 metres in length were in danger of defaulting on their loans. Local news reports from 1998 suggest that about 10 per cent of the fleet was sold during this period and that most of the sales were an attempt to forestall bankruptcy proceedings.

CONCLUSION

In this chapter, the ways in which gender intersects with the process of production in the fishing community of the Bigoudennie have been described. The process of production has been widely defined to include the reproduction of labour power in the home (in terms of both new labourers and the rejuvenation of current labour power), the economic maintenance of the family-based fishing enterprises, and the subsistence of the household itself. The households represented by Jeanne, Marie, and Pascale—representing the situation of a big boat skipper's wife, a small boat skipper's wife, and the wife of a deckhand—are typical of the household of fisherfolk in the Bigouden fishery. In each case, the economic importance of the women's paid and unpaid labour power is critical in the maintenance of the household unit. Their individual stories highlight the fact that, despite their common experience as women, their day-to-day lives are materially different as a result of the economic differences between their households. As we have seen, there are real material differences between households depending on whether they own a fishboat or not. In the following chapter I return to the work world of men to examine in greater detail the social divisions between boat owner and crew. Here the economic basis for the differences between households is examined at the level of the social reproduction of the unit of production intergenerationally.

6

THE DIFFERENCE A FAMILY MAKES

OCIAL RELATIONS BETWEEN MEN onboard fishing boats and women's work ashore are important aspects of the material conditions of Bigouden fisherfolk's social world. And, while union organizers may invoke the image of the family to describe social relations between skippers and crews, it is in fact the family as a social institution that to a large extent makes the technical process of fishing possible.

In this chapter, we shift to the consideration of a sequence of stories of family,[1] work, and the everyday. These stories document "lived" histories, which are intermingled with and simultaneously oppose and affirm the broader history of the place. While the family histories related here can in some sense be generalized across the spectrum of fisherfolk in the Bigoudennie, they are primarily stories of families who own fishboats.

Labour within the household and family is necessarily rigidly segregated by gender. The material reality of fishing in the Bigoudennie removes men from the home on a practically permanent basis. The administration and maintenance of the household, including the care of children, lies firmly within the domain of the fisherman's wife and other female kinfolk.

The exclusion of women from harvesting fish, while by no means quantitatively accurate (as we saw in Chapter Five, there are three women registered as fishers out of a total of 1,600 in Le Guilvinec, one of whom operates her own small vessel and sells her fish directly to consumers), is however, a social reality in that women are widely believed to be ill-suited for fishing. This is

---

[1] In keeping with standard anthropological practice, in order to preserve their anonymity, these families are identified only by pseudonyms and, where necessary, certain identifying details have been altered.

despite the fact that, as the few women who are in the fishery demonstrate, there is no physical reason to prevent them from doing so. However, as I have noted elsewhere, the exclusion of women from fishing is tied tightly to male conceptions of masculinity, which "are strongly linked to defining 'their' occupation as being a male occupation in which women are, by definition, unable to participate" (Menzies 1991, 15; cf. Binkley 1995).[2]

Underlying and connecting the stories of work and family are themes of separation between fisher and partner, parent and child. For the men, work histories are recited in terms of the names of the boats they owned or fished on and the names of the skippers; for the women, the stories revolve around work in the home, caring for children, and balancing house and boat budgets.

The two case studies related here detail the different occupational trajectories of skippers and crews. They also address the question of the difference that family makes in staying in fishing or being pushed out. The first case, Luc and Martine Kernevad, is of a deckhand's family. The second case is of a boat owner's family.

LUC AND MARTINE KERNEVAD

I met Luc for the first time during a fishers' protest in late 1994. As I got to know him, he told me about his life working on the fish boats. "At the age of 15 I went to sea on the dragger *New Times*,[3] a wooden boat of 17 metres, equipped for deep-sea fishing. The trips were 10–15 days off the coast of England and Ireland. There were seven men in the crew. We worked between 18 and 20 hours a day. My job consisted of cooking, stacking the langoustine, and threading the net-mending needles with twine. The job pleases me, but it is hard and very tiring."

The families of both Luc and Martine are native Bigouden. They have lived in the region for generation upon generation going back beyond the point of it making any sense to talk of their arrival. However, one risks accepting a false sense of continuity in employment when, from the vantage point of the present, we trace backwards a linear progression to some distant ancestor. Luc himself reckons his lineage patrilineally. He is at least the fifth generation of the family Kernevad to have made his living as a fisher, and he is

---

[2] The question of women's involvement has been discussed in two important collections: Nadel-Klein and Davis 1988; and Allison, Jacobs, and Porter 1989. See also Cole 1991.

[3] The skipper of the boat was his father's brother. To respect the anonymity of the respondents, the name of the boat has been changed.

TABLE 6.1

Employment categories of Luc Kernevad's generation

Position relation	Fisher	Fish worker	Other blue collar	Professional	Service	Not known
Cousin	2	3	3	2	5	2
Sibling	0	2	0	1	2	0

likely to be the last. Of Luc's siblings, none currently work as fishers—two are in jobs connected with the fishery, and three work in areas completely separated from fishing. Of 17 cousins, only five work in fisheries-related jobs (two as fishers, one a ship's carpenter, and two in machine shops).

However, depending upon whether one considers the progression of the family lineally (from child to grandparent) or laterally generation by generation (sibling to sibling, cousin to cousin), the family's occupational image changes. To say Luc comes from a family of fishers is to privilege the occupation of his father, grandfather, and great-grandfather over, say, his mother's father or his great-aunt on his mother's side (the first was a liveryman, the second ran a small farm with her husband). It is also to ignore the peasant pre-history that moved between sea and land as well as the lateral shifts out of fishing in each generation. It is more accurate, therefore, to suggest that Luc's family was part of the rural proletariat and took up jobs when and where they could. During the period in which the fishery grew, his family members became fishers.

Martine's family represents an entirely different segment of the social matrix than Luc's. The dominant occupation in her family has been peasant agriculture. Martine worked on the farm as a young child. At 15, she found a factory job in a nearby town. None of her sisters married farmers, nor did her brothers choose to become one. Of her siblings, she is the only one still living in the Bigoudennie.

Martine and Luc currently live in a house built on a section of her family's 20-hectare farm, a farm which has been held in the family for at least three generations. No one in her family is currently farming the land. Some has been sold for housing, about 6 hectares are sitting fallow, and the remaining 12 or so are leased to a local dairy farmer who has a milk quota. Martine's parents went to their graves farming the land. They actively encouraged their children to find jobs in the fishery or in the towns.

Luc has maintained an impressive work history, crewing on only five boats over the past 25 years. After fishing for several years with his uncle, he took a job on a modern deep-sea dragger in the 24-metre class. He switched boats once in the mid-1980s to take a better job and then switched again in the early 1990s (just before the crisis) to a coastal dragger, wanting to be closer to his children during their adolescence. Coastal draggers, 12–23 metres in length, typically fish day trips and usually return to port by the late afternoon. During certain seasons some of these boats switch to three- to five-day trips. Luc changed boats again in 1998 to a boat that fishes only day trips. "I'm getting a bit old for longer trips," he explained.

Martine worked in the same factory until the birth of her first child. At points when Luc's income fell off (most notably during the crisis of the early 1990s), she found employment in a variety of short-term jobs such as cleaning and clerking. Both Luc and Martine hope their children find employment outside of the fishing industry since "there's no future in the fishery for a young man." Their son Yves recently completed technical college and in September 2000 began working as an apprentice in a service-sector trade. Their daughter Annie is almost finished her training as a childcare worker. Even as the fishery has entered a period of economic recovery, Luc and Martine are pleased that their son and daughter have found occupations beyond fishing.

GILBERT AND CATHERINE BAZHAD

The personal and family histories of Gilbert and Catherine Bazhad are intimately entwined with the history of the Bigoudennie. Gilbert, born in the fishing village of Léchiagat (just across the harbour from Le Guilvinec), descends from a paternal line of fisherfolk that disappears beyond the scope of living memory. Catherine, born in the village of St. Guénolé, has inherited a patrimony equally as rooted in the maritime milieu. As a couple, they have maintained their kindred's involvement in the fishing industry.

Gilbert's work history cuts through the period of social transformation following the Second World War. He started fishing at the age of 14 on his father's sardine seiner out of Le Guilvinec. After three years of learning the trade, he switched to trawling as a deckhand aboard his uncle's boat. In the 1950s, many young men went to work aboard the growing distant-water fleet; Gilbert was no exception.

When Gilbert left the Bigoudennie in 1955 to fish on the distant-water trawlers, his father retired and passed on the running of the family boat to Gilbert's older brother André. After three years working in the offshore fleet, Gilbert returned to the Bigoudennie, married Catherine, and went to work

TABLE 6.2

Gilbert Bazhad's work history

Year	Position	Owner and type of boat fished on
1950	Mousse (inbreaker)	Father's boat, fishing sardines out of Le Guilvinec.
1953	Deckhand	Father's brother's boat, side-trawler fishing out of Le Guilvinec.
1955	Deckhand/bosun	Distant-water trawler fishing out of Lorient.
1958	Mate	Father's brother's boat, side-trawler fishing out of Le Guilvinec.
1963	Skipper	Partnership with his two brothers, built new wooden boat for side trawling, fishing out of Le Guilvinec.
1968	Skipper	Bought out brothers' share of boat.
1977	Skipper	Built new steel stern trawler, sons listed as co-owners.
1983	Skipper	Built second steel stern trawler, eldest son operates boat built in 1977.
1988	Retired	1977 vessel replaced with a new steel stern trawler, oldest son runs new boat, second son takes over boat built in 1983; retains ownership interest in both vessels.

on his uncle's wooden side trawler. As his uncle had no sons to take over his boat, Gilbert was hired as the mate. As his uncle approached retirement age (52–55), Gilbert assumed greater responsibilities on the boat and, by 1960, was practically running the boat as his own. His uncle retired and sold the boat in 1963, causing Gilbert to commission the building of a new wooden trawler.

From 1963, when he bought his first boat, to his retirement in 1988, Gilbert was involved in building four new vessels (one wood, three steel). He formed a partnership with his two brothers in 1963. André continued to run the family boat, replacing it with a new vessel in 1964. His youngest brother Jean-Pierre, who had been working on the uncle's boat, came to the new boat with Gilbert and fished with him until the mid-1980s when he retired early for medical reasons.

Throughout this, Catherine worked primarily in the home. She was responsible for maintaining the boat accounts, arranging provisions, and ensuring that payment deadlines were kept. Often hidden from view, this work is as important in the maintenance and perpetuation of the fishing enterprise as was Gilbert's ability to make deals and catch fish.

According to Catherine, men have a hard time with money. "They go from their mother's home to their wife's home," she said. "We do it all for them. They can't even write a cheque! Without a good woman—one who knows that it is important he spend a little in the bistro, not too much, just enough to waste—he'll waste it all."

Catherine began work as a cannery worker in her home town, St. Guénolé. She worked there for five years. In addition to running a household and managing a fishing enterprise, she also crocheted items, which she sold at the local markets. Like many other young women of her time, she had worn a coiffe but, by the early 1960s, had traded it in for a "modern" hairstyle. "My mother and grandmother wore a coiffe every day of the week," Catherine said. "I did as a young woman but stopped when I started doing our accounts. It just didn't seem practical anymore." Her daughter, Annie, belongs to a local folk group. She now wears the coiffe to special events, festivals, and the occasional performance.

To locate an occupation other than fishing in either Catherine's or Gilbert's family tree one must go back beyond the 1860s. Of the eight "ancestral households" economically active in 1860, two involve peasant agriculture with small-scale fishing and one unambiguously derived its livelihood from peasant agriculture. Of the generation immediately prior to the 1860 generation, Gilbert and Catherine said that about half were peasants. The others combined fishing and agriculture.

As presented here, only those in a direct line to (and from) Gilbert and Catherine are represented in the kinship diagram. This creates the possibility, as discussed in the section above, of generating a false image of continuity. The powerful aspect of this family is the extent to which nearly five generations have been involved in the fishery. Although as detailed a genealogical study as that by Martine Segalen in *Fifteen Generations of Bretons* (1991) is not the primary purpose of this project, several observations about patterns of marriage and their relevance for keeping vessels and workers "inside" the fishery can be suggested.

In her study of kinship in the Bigoudennie, Segalen carefully describes a system of affinal-linking marriages, which over the course of several generations knit kindreds together. She suggests that these linking marriages (which have no emic designation) function to maintain property within the "family" (1991). The density of fishing occupations within Gilbert and Catherine's family suggest the possibility that linking marriages such as those iden-

TABLE 6.3

Catherine Bazhad's work history

Year	Position	Comments
1954	Cannery worker	St. Guénolé, seasonal work.
1958		Moved to Le Guilvinec following marriage to Gilbert.
1959	"Femme de ménage"	Following the birth of their first child, Catherine stopped working in the paid workforce, working instead in the home.
1963	Bookkeeper/manager	Following the purchase of a new boat, Catherine was responsible for keeping the vessel's accounts. As the enterprise developed, she became the virtual manager of the family enterprise.
1988	"Retired"	Ceased active involvement in the fishing enterprise, much of her work having been taken over by her eldest son's wife during the 1980s.

tified by Segalen were used to keep boats within male kindreds. Based on the data collected from 20 fishing families and extending back three to five generations, there is strong evidence to suggest that, at least in terms of work opportunities and partnerships, the typical relationship was between agnatic kin, specifically father–son, uncle–nephew, or brother–brother. Up until the mid-1980s, most crews were agnatically based groups of fathers, brothers, and uncles. A second important link is that between a man and his father-in-law, perhaps representing a transfer of a woman's share of the estate from father to son-in-law.

Based on three generations of men from Gilbert and Catherine's family, I examined the kin relationship between a young man and the boat skipper on his first fishing trip. Based on 21 "first trips" it is evident that the preferred situation is to first go to sea on one's father's or uncle's boat (see Table 6.4). To further refine this picture, I then compared the kin relations between boat-partnerships. Here the picture shifts somewhat. Joint investments are almost as common with one's father-in-law as with one's agnatic kin (see Table 6.5).

The data are limited by the manner in which they were collected. This restricts, to a certain extent, the ability to effectively generalize beyond the specific cases described. Information was collected from the core group of fishers with whom I worked. No effort was made to generate a "random sample." Instead, I employed a "snowball" technique in which the fishers'

TABLE 6.4

Skipper's family connection to young fisher on his first fishing job

First fishing job, skipper's relationship to young fisher	Number of occurrences in sample, n = 21
Father	7
Father's brother	5
Father's father	3
Brother	1
Cousin (father's side)	2
Cousin (mother's side)	0
Mother's brother	2
Mother's father	1

TABLE 6.5

Boat-owning partnerships and family relations

Family relationship of boat-ownership partner	Number of occurrences in sample, n = 11
Father	2
Father's brother	1
Father's father	0
Brother	3
Cousin (father's side)	0
Cousin (mother's side)	0
Mother's brother	0
Mother's father	0
Father-in-law	3
Brother-in-law	2

own social networks were used to recruit respondents. Although I am reasonably certain that the data represent an accurate overview of the social world within which Bigouden fishing skippers operate, they do not necessarily represent a statistical description of the world of French fishers.

In conducting occupational genealogies, I realized early on that there is an important difference between the history of crewing and joint ownership within families such as the Bazhads and the histories of families of crewmembers like the Kernevads. Crewmember families display a greater heterogeneity in employment terms than do boat owners, a situation that can be traced over several generations. Furthermore, there is a lower rate of retention in the fishery among the crewmembers' families than in the boat-owner families. This tends to suggest that some of the manoeuvres of families with respect to conserving property had the impact of creating social barriers between crew and skipper, which are to a large extent "masked" by the relative egalitarianism of shipboard life. It was occasionally noted in interviews, for example, that skippers' wives and crewmembers' wives did not associate and that, in times of crisis, this intensified the social problems in the community. There has clearly been a difference in income between skippers and crews, and their social interests are indeed different and at times antagonistic.

FAMILIES AND THE MAINTENANCE OF PROPERTY

In preparing for fieldwork in the Bigoudennie, I had noted that a major shift was occurring in the structure of employment opportunities in the French fishing industry. Between the 1950s and 1993, the number of Breton fishers had dropped from 25,000 to 8,000. In order to understand how fisherfolk were surviving—or failing to survive—I planned to compare two groups of respondents. The primary group would be selected from among fishers and their families whose base of operations was in the port of Le Guilvinec. The second group was to be composed of former fishers and their family members. This was initially conceived of in terms of men being pushed off the boats into waged labour either in or outside the region. To a certain extent, these expectations were confirmed by the occupational genealogies that I completed.

My speculations about workers leaving fishing stemmed from the experience of commercial fishers in British Columbia where, following licensing changes introduced in the herring and halibut fisheries during the 1980s, there was an obvious and easily measurable decrease in jobs. Men who had fished since childhood were made redundant and were forced, if they were able, to seek employment in other areas. However, the shift out of fishing in France occurred long before the men ever reached the boats.

In the postwar period, a new openness in the educational system allowed more working-class and peasant families to give their children a post-secondary education. In the context of the expanding welfare state, jobs were plentiful. Added to this was a dramatic change in family size: in one generation family size dropped from between five and nine children to between two and four. In the occupational genealogies collected during my fieldwork, a move away from manual labour toward white-collar employment based outside of the region was evident. As my work progressed, I realized that those who had kept a foothold in the fishery were predominantly those whose families had owned fishboats for a generation or more.

The potential problem of displaced fishers also seems to be controlled through the educational system. As with many other occupations in France, one must attend a specialized school to become certified as a fisher. Advancement from deckhand to mate or mechanic, or from mate to skipper, requires additional certificates. French fishers can also retire after 37.5 years of work to a full pension (the minimum reported pension was US$1,750 per month). The official age of retirement for French mariners is 55.[4] Understandably, men over the age of 55 are rare indeed onboard a French fishing boat. Thus, potential surplus labour is siphoned off by a system of early retirement and is further inhibited through restricted enrollments at the special fishing schools.

The family histories related in this chapter encapsulate and express the difference a family makes in maintaining a foothold in the Bigouden fishing industry. They emphasize how individuals and their kin have negotiated their way through the morass of social transformations and upheavals that have characterized this region. In recounting these two types of history— the history of things, such as boats, fleets, and gear, and the history of families—I wish to emphasize the interconnectedness and the messiness of everyday life.

One of the more revealing aspects of the two family histories is the difference between families who have managed to maintain vessel ownership through several generations and those who have not. As property owners in control of a rather tenuous and risky enterprise, families worked hard to conserve the capital necessary for vessel ownership within the family. This is not a feature of vessel ownership unique to the Bigoudennie. In my earlier work with British Columbian fishers (Menzies 1992; 1993), I discussed the perpetuation of ownership in terms of the difference between simple and expanded reproduction.

Under conditions of simple reproduction, the fishing enterprise maintains one unit of production. The capital investment may necessarily increase, but the effect is the same: an enterprise sufficient to support a fisher and his

---

[4] France increased the minimum age of retirement for most sectors in 2010. Certain sectors, such as fisheries, the military, and police, were exempt from the new law.

family. Under conditions of expanded reproduction, the fishing enterprise increases not just in terms of capital investment but also in terms of the number of productive units.

What is interesting about artisanal fishing is that typically, even under conditions of expanded reproduction, there eventually comes a point at which the enterprise either hives off into two or more smaller ones or makes a qualitative leap into becoming a "fully capitalist firm." Thus, it is quite likely that at some time in the near future, Gilbert Bazhad's sons will formally separate their enterprises and concentrate on accumulating sufficient capital to assist their own sons' move into the fishery. It is possible, however, that the Bazhad fishing enterprise will jump the barrier between simple commodity production and become a firm. There are currently only two such enterprises in the Bigoudennie. One has eight 24-metre draggers and the other has five.

The crewmembers' families move through a field of employment opportunities simultaneously more tenuous (owning productive property does make a difference) and more open. It is more tenuous than that faced by their boat-owning neighbours because they are solely reliant upon being able to sell their labour power in order to survive. It is more open in that their concerns have less to do with maintaining control within the kindred over productive property and more with locating employment for kindred members.

The social transformations that have swept through this region have inscribed themselves into the tissue of family histories. Children in families without access to productive property tend to move into other careers outside the fishery. Those with productive property favour marriages with other boat-owning families. In a very real sense, the peasant past is reproduced in the struggle to maintain a foothold in the fishery.

CONCLUSION

THE WORLD OF COMMERCIAL FISHERS seems to sustain just one thing: crisis. The response to crisis can vary from passive resistance to open revolt. In the Bigoudennie, a detailed history of active resistance can be traced back from contemporary social protests to the revolutionary trade unionism of the early twentieth century and the even more remote anti-feudal peasant revolt of 1675. Each of these moments of struggle has left its imprint on the collective memory and, for better or worse, has laid the pathways of resistance to the contemporary period of neo-liberal globalization.

One of capitalism's defining features is its inherent capacity for change, destruction, and recomposition. This constant process of pulling down and building back up has important consequences for class, ethnic, and local identities. In the borderlands of Europe's internal colonies and along the margins of Euro-American settler society, capitalism has been engaged in a spatial and cultural restructuring with critical consequences. During the early period of industrial transformation in the Bigoudennie (roughly 1880–1914), local resistance was expressed as class struggle. It was represented symbolically in the red flag and the singing of the *Internationale*. Following the collapse of the sardine fishery in the early part of the twentieth century, a local "Bigouden" identity took precedence over that of being a "worker." This metaphoric shift serves to conceal, or even displace discursively, the underlying class dynamics of the artisanal fishery in which the economic survival of boat owners is to some extent dependent upon their ability to exploit the social labour of their own kin.

The local manifestations of new sets of identities that emerged in the Bigoudennie out of the encounter between the larger (that is, the world capitalist system) and the local was dependent on the nature of the overarching state formation and the pre-existing social formation. The Bigoudennie was an economically stagnant agricultural region in which the rural peasantry were barely eking out a living when industrial capitalism arrived in much the same manner as it was implanted in Europe's overseas colonies. That is, it was brought into the backcountry of Brittany by outside capitalists who expropriated local labour and resources and undermined local forms of production. The resulting form of struggle reflects this almost colonial context. This is not to say that it was explicitly or necessarily nationalist in nature. In truth, nationalist sentiment seems never to have moved far beyond simple resentments commonly expressed by hinterland peoples toward the urban centre. Rather, local expressions of class solidarity were more easily cultivated because the cannery owners and managers were French-speaking and the working class was Breton-speaking. This, in combination with the transition from peasant to industrial conditions of work, created the context for strong collective action and militant trade unionism.

As opposed to more clearly nationalist "Breton" movements described by McDonald (1989), contemporary Bigouden militants see their struggle as one based on maintaining the viability of their "community" but not as part of a struggle for autonomy or independence (see also Le Coadic 2003). Here, idioms of "locality" and "community" are used as a medium to articulate specific class demands and viewpoints within a context in which representations of class have become despatialized.

In examining the twinned issues of livelihood and resistance, Gavin Smith describes how cultures of opposition that are based in the local or in expressions of "community" can be seen to sow "the seeds for a more broadly based oppositional class consciousness" (1989, 236). Following Sabean (1984), Smith defines community "not [as a set of] shared values or common understanding, so much as the fact that members of a community are engaged in the same argument, the same *raisonnement*, the same *Rede*, the same discourse, in which alternative strategies, misunderstandings, conflicting goals and values are threshed out.... What makes community is the discourse" (1989, 29–30). In the Breton illustration, it is interesting to note that identities based in the local or the "community" have (re)emerged as the primary expression of class interests, whereas Smith was documenting a case in which he saw the local culture of opposition as forming a basis upon which a more generalized class consciousness might emerge.

The more abstract notion of being "Breton" appeals to a cultural "quest for authentic identity" (Badone 1992, 808; see also Le Coadic 2003) in which pan-Celtic celebrations of traditional costumes, dance, and music play an important part. Yet the majority of the Bigouden fishers support "French" political parties on the national plane as opposed to regionally based groupings advocating autonomy or independence. At the very least, this points to the complexity and divergence of social identities in which a fisher may well be "Bigouden" at the demonstration, "Breton" at the local *Kermesse* or festival, and "French" on election day.

The early struggles brought people together in an industrial setting who, until that point, had primarily thought of themselves as villagers rather than in the more abstract as French, Breton, or worker. In their struggle against the "bosses" of the late nineteenth and early twentieth centuries, their own collective identity, manifest in a class idiom, emerged. Though not evident at the time, this early proletarian identity contained within it the potential of transmutation into an ethnic or "local" identity. Subsequent changes in the local political economy—primarily the collapse of the industrial canning industry—stripped away the unambiguous class basis of their collective identity and opened the path for the emergence of a *Bigouden* identity. The fishing skippers of the 1990s then attempted to manage this identity in order to advance their own specific set of class interests.

In this book I have retold the story of a group of people struggling to maintain their foothold in a way of life based on family-owned fishing vessels. Fishers, especially those owning boats, are in the middle of a major social transformation, which has the potential to utterly change the way in which they and their families live. Their response to this crisis—the social protest movement of the mid-1990s—was fundamentally conservative in that it tried to maintain the status quo, which was based on a world defined in national or local economic terms, that is, a world in which the nation-state had the political and economic ability to effectively control its own economy. However, if the post-*somethingists* are correct in any sense, it is in recognizing the effective globalization of the contemporary world system within which the power of the regionally based nation-state to effectively and decisively control its internal economy has become seriously compromised. Yet, and this is the paradox, the French state and the EU have increased their specific interventions into and control over the harvesting of fish. Fishers thus face greater economic uncertainty combined with increased control over their harvesting operations. It is within this changed context that the struggle of the boat owners to maintain their individual fishing enterprises is, in all of its irony, perhaps one of the last "Luddite" struggles of the Euro-American world.

THE ARGUMENT

This book is ultimately concerned with how family-based fishing enterprises continue in the face of what seem to be overwhelming odds. This has been accomplished through a historical ethnography of the fishers—skippers, crews, and their families—who make the Bigouden region in France their home. While I am ultimately concerned with all Bigouden fishers, this analysis has primarily focused on skipper/boat owners and the manner through and by which this group of productive petty bourgeoisie organize their enterprises and cultivate community-based alliances in a struggle to survive despite the massive social transformations now occurring in the European fisheries.

Two important conclusions emerge from this study. The first details the specific ways in which the development of the welfare state reconfigured the social-spatial dimensions of class struggle. The second concerns the issue of custom, struggle, and invention. Here, I am specifically referring to the manner in which a unique cultural particularity emerged out of the imposition of industrial social relations, specifically, the development of the local Bigouden coiffe. The crucial issue is the manner in which a seemingly archaic custom was in fact a direct product of the experience of **proletarianization** even as it became entangled in the present within a social protest rooted in the productive middle classes.

STATE AND SOCIAL CLASS

The development of the French welfare state, especially in its postwar Gaullist form, coincided with the decline of the industrial sardine canning industry and the rise of an artisanal fishery of skipper/boat owners. The state was a conscious actor in this process of transformation. The archival evidence is clear. Capital and state did in fact combine to undermine relations of social solidarity within the fishers' communities and to pull certain classes of fishers into the orbit of the propertied classes. It is important to emphasize that the form of state intervention was neither limited to nor uniquely focused on the use of coercive force—indeed, coercive force scarcely enters into the construction of this social "order." More importantly, the development of state-funded financial instruments (i.e., the Crédit Maritime, a credit union–like agency) deliberately targeted segments of the fishing communities (specifically, skippers) in order to incorporate them into the capitalist economy through the device of ownership. The process of economic globalization in the late twentieth century coincided with the weakening of the French state's capacity to control local economic conditions and its increasing efforts to regulate how fishers carried out their daily fishing activities. As a result, artisanal fishers came to view the regulatory framework of the French state and the EU as the primary target of their political actions.

LOCAL CUSTOM AND SOCIAL STRUGGLE

The question of how local customs fit into social struggle is particularly important. In the Bigoudennie, the lace coiffe emerged as a symbol of local identity at precisely the moment when the local society was undergoing a transition from a peasant to a capitalist economy. The structure of social inequality changed from one in which the primary lines of control over labour were located within the family to an industrial waged economy in which the previous kin-based forms of control were disrupted. As noted earlier, the old paternalism of the "father" was replaced by a "new" paternalism in which the manager or owner of the cannery now appropriated the labour power of household members.

This new form of social inequality had different meanings for the genders. Men working on the fishboats were nominally independent of the direct control of industrial capital over their labour. They experienced a work setting in which the idiom of companionship and equality predominated (though, as pointed out in Chapters Four and Five, the control of a skipper over the labour of his crew throughout the twentieth century is similar to the control of a factory boss over a wage labourer). Women, however, worked under the direct control of capital. They were paid wages based on their hours of work and, for the most part, worked in an assembly-line setting. Thus, the experiences of industrial capitalism varied dramatically according to one's gender.

In the face of constant change, three enduring features are crucial to note: (1) the language of the local, or the construction of a local identity, is part of a structure of conflicting class antagonisms that crosscut families; (2) the symbolism of struggle in the 1990s was local but the arena of struggle was not—struggle has become located in the despatialized context of the universalization of production and exchange; and (3) the most influential speakers are the boat owners who, through their skillful use of local identity and the shared memory of struggle, have been able to forge an effective political coalition with their crews, the crews' families, and a national social democratic agenda that has primarily benefited the most successful boat owners.

The struggles during the Sardine Years at the beginning of the twentieth century centred around the extension of capitalist relations of production into a previously agrarian society. Between then and the 1990s yet another, potentially more fundamental, shift has occurred. This shift is not epochal, nor is it a harbinger of some new stage of the world economy. Rather, it represents the universalization of capitalist relations of production. In this context, fisheries are subordinated to an economic logic that extends far beyond the local fish port, auction, or fishing ground. It is in this newly emerging global capitalist system (as opposed to a world economic system whose dynamic rests on trade and exchange) that the local identity "Bigouden" has emerged as part of a tactical program for political struggle. Thus, the boat owners attempt to strategically place themselves within an intensely local construction while simultaneously orienting or locating their field of struggle within a global frame. In so doing, they try to turn the experience of past resistance to the use of the present. But in this struggle between the remembered past and the desired future, one wonders if the fishers of the Bigoudennie will manage to survive their own present.

THE FUTURE OF THE BIGOUDEN FISHERY

While producing the film *Weather the Storm*, a documentary about the Bigouden fisheries in the context of economic globalization, I asked local fishermen, government officials, academics, and politicians if there was a future for the Bigouden artisanal fisheries. With one notable exception they all said emphatically "Yes!"

The exception was Amboise Guellec, a long-time conservative politician in the region, who said that while one "might regret the loss of our marine folklore, fishermen had to focus on managing their business and rationalizing their production" (quoted in Menzies and Rashleigh 2008). For Guellec, the artisanal fishery was an archaic institution that was neither economically nor ecologically viable. My research in the Bigoudennie, however, suggests the opposite, that is, that artisanal fishers are in fact more economically and ecologically sustainable than fisheries that scale up and take on the form of capitalist firms (Menzies and Rashleigh 2008). However, the future of this fishery cannot be predicted by recourse to abstract laws of development or the lessons of history. The outcome is contingent upon the ever-present struggle, that awkward dance between structure and agency that dogs human history.

Politicians such as Amboise Guellec actively call for a transformation of fisheries to become more capitalistic. Fishermen leaders such as André Le Berre (one of the leaders of the struggles in the mid-1990s) and Robert Bou-ghéon (current president of the CLPM) argue that there is a place for artisanal

FIGURE 7.1: Returning to port at the end of a day of fishing, Le Guilvinec

fisheries in France and in the world. The life work of these men has been geared toward supporting and advancing an artisanal way of life. Along with their fellow fishermen and neighbours in the Bigoudennie, they are actively engaged in making their own history. While they do not choose the conditions under which they struggle, they are taking action in a world too often held back by apathy and cynicism.

EACH TIME I RETURN to the Bigoudennie, I find my friend Jean-Jacques is still fishing. "One more year," he keeps telling me. When he does finally retire, Jean-Jacques will be the last of his family to make a living from the sea. "It is a hard life," he says, but it is also "a life filled with rewards, with the true pleasure in the work." Even as his time in fishing comes to a close, he and his fellow Bigouden fishers envision a future for artisanal fisheries in the Bigoudennie. I share their hope. Ultimately, it is a decision that the Bigouden fishers must make anew each day. To be an artisanal fisher is, as René-Pierre Chever says, a "permanent struggle" (quoted in Menzies and Rashleigh 2008), but it is a struggle worth taking on!

GLOSSARY

Amorique: The Latin name for Brittany.

artisanal fishery: A fishery that is primarily performed by family-owned fishing vessels. The size of artisanal fishboats and fisheries varies in size and scope globally. Some artisanal fisheries operate from small human-powered skiffs or even from shore stations. In France and other countries, artisanal fisheries may involve vessels up to 15–20 metres in length. Onboard work relations are often mediated by kin-relationships and tend to be more collegial than work relations in a factory. (See also **simple commodity production.**)

Bigoudennie: The region on the westernmost edge of Brittany that forms the primary fieldsite of this ethnography. (The adjective Bigouden refers to this district.)

Briezh: The Breton name for Brittany.

capitalism: A mode of production in which two primary social classes exist—those who own businesses and the rest who own nothing but their own labour power. Under the capitalist mode of production most social relations are defined by a cash relationship. Advocates of capitalism argue that only through a free market can true freedom exist. Freedom is defined as having the potential (though not necessarily the capacity) to buy anything that one might want. In practical terms, capitalism creates the conditions under which massive global poverty and social inequality continue unabated.

catching capacity: The potential amount of fish that a particular vessel or type of fishing gear can harvest in a given period of time operating without restraint.

coiffe: French term for the lace bonnets and headdresses that form part of the traditional costume of the Bigouden region.

Comité local des pêches maritimes (CLPM): The official representative organization of fishers and fish processes at the local level in France. The CLPM is a quasi-governmental organization that provides for communication from the fisheries sector directly into the government and delivers services to the fisheries sector at the local level.

Comité national des pêches maritimes et des élevages marins (CNPMEM): The official representative organization of fishers and fish processes at the national level. The CNPMEM is a quasi-governmental organization that provides for communication from the fisheries sector directly into the government.

commodity: Something that has been produced by human labour, which is then exchanged for other commodities in a free market. Money is a special type of commodity that allows for the universal translation of other commodities such as food, clothing, fish, and boats into comparable units.

Common Fisheries Policy (CFP): EU regulatory framework, first established in 1982, that governs fisheries within the common oceans of the EU. The CFP sets total allowable catches of all commercially harvested fish species and regulates the types of fishing gear and the numbers of fishboats that each of the member nations of the EU can operate.

corporatism: An approach to economic governance that tries to unite labour, business, and government in the regulation of industry. In France this has its roots in Marshal Pétain's Vichy labour code. Pétain was the head of state of the collaborationist French government that surrendered to and then co-operated with Germany in 1940–44.

division of the catch: See entry under share agreement.

division of labour: Refers to the ways in which production and work are divided among social groups. In fishing communities, for example, labour is often divided by gender: men will do one part of the work (typically catching fish) and women another (typically in the cannery). Division of labour can also refer to how the specific process of work is broken down into separate components. For example, on a fishboat there is a division of labour between the skipper who operates the fishing boat, the deckhands who do the basic work involved in operating the fishing machinery and putting the fish into the fish hold, and the engineer who is responsible for taking care of the boat's main engine or other machinery onboard.

dragger: See entry under trawlers.

European Union (EU): A supra-national organization of European nations. The EU is governed by the European Commission (the executive council of the EU), the European Parliament (members of which are directly elected by European citizens), and the Council of the European Union (representing the governments of member nations).

field: In anthropological terms the field is the place where one goes to conduct anthropological research. For contemporary anthropologists the field can be as varied as the virtual spaces of online chat groups to distant remote locations or the coffee shop near one's home. This is quite different from early-twentieth-century anthropologists who considered the field to be a remote location inhabited by non-Western peoples.

fieldwork: The term anthropologists use to describe their research in the field.

fish auction (*la criée*): Fresh fish are sold daily in each of the Bigouden fish-ports. In Le Guilvinec, the daily auction takes on a carnivalesque air as tourists gather to watch the boats arriving in the late afternoon for the evening fish auction. A quick search of the Internet under *Retour de pêche* will bring up dozens of photos of Breton boats heading into the auction house.

fishing gear: Nets, traps, lines, and other devices used for catching fish. The major types of fishing gear used in the Bigouden fishery include the following:

gillnet: A net made of fine twine that is hard for fish to see. The net is set in a straight line across the path of the fish, which become entangled in the net by their gills.

longline: A hook-and-line fishery. Longlines can be set along the bottom of the ocean to catch cod or other bottom-dwelling fish. This gear can also be used with floats to catch fish such as tuna.

seine: A net that is set around schools of fish and then drawn together to form a bag that traps the fish. Seines are used to catch fish such as sardines and herring.

trap: Primarily used to catch crabs and spiny lobsters. Only a handful of boats use traps in the Bigoudennie.

trawl: A bag-like net that is pulled behind the fish boat, normally along the bottom of the ocean. This is the primary fishing gear used in the Bigouden fishery and is used to catch all manner of finfish, crustaceans, and langoustines.

flexible accumulation: A system of capitalist accumulation described by David Harvey in *The Condition of Postmodernity* (1989) as combining new technologies of production with changes in labour practices. Computers that mediate production and inventory systems make it possible for firms to restructure production spatially and temporally. For example, electronic components, produced in a range of factories and workshops spread around the world, are assembled in another plant. Using computer inventory systems, parts required for final assembly can be produced just in time for their use, thereby reducing the cost to firms of holding large inventories of parts in advance of needing them. As opposed to the Fordist system of manufacturing that involved regularized labour forces and thus created large workforces in a single location, flexible accumulation distributes production spatially in such a manner as to undermine the capacity of working people to control their immediate working conditions.

Food and Agriculture Organization (FAO) of the United Nations (UN): The UN's lead organization in the struggle to end global hunger.

Force of Order (Compagnies républicaines de sécurité–CRS): A French paramilitary anti-riot police force created in 1944. It is one of two national anti-riot forces in France, which are often mistaken for each other. The other force, the Gendarmerie Mobile, dates back to the nineteenth century and originally functioned as an infantry. In recent years, the national government has begun the process of integrating the two forces into one organization, given the overlap of their functions.

de Gaulle, Charles: Second World War general and hero of the Free French Army who was the leader of the Provisional Government of the French Republic and who became the first president of the reconstituted Fifth Republic of France in 1959. De Gaulle was a political conservative whose followers maintained and implemented corporatist policies to manage France's economy.

gillnet: See entry under **fishing gear**.

la grève (strikes): An organized withdrawal of labour or a work stoppage by working people to effect an improvement in their wages and/or conditions of work. Sometimes strikes can take on revolutionary implications when they extend beyond the immediate economic needs of working people and challenge political elites. France has a history in which economic struggles have transformed into political struggles that have led to changes in government and to democratic rights for the entire citizenry.

Hélias, Pierre-Jakez: Noted Breton author of *The Horse of Pride* (1978), which documents the day-to-day life of Breton peasants in early-twentieth-century Bigoudennie.

industrial fishery: There is no generally agreed-upon definition of what might constitute an industrial fishery. In this book it is used to refer to the way in which production is organized. Industrial fisheries are thus those in which machine production takes precedence over human or animal labour in all aspects of the fishery. It is also one in which the primary form of ownership is corporate. Thus, in this book, what makes the sardine fishery industrial is the manner by which the processing of the fish is organized in fish factories, while, at the same time, the harvesting remains artisanal in that individual fishermen own the boats. Today, many fisheries exhibit characteristics that are both industrial and artisanal in that harvesting tends to be by individual boat owners while processing and distribution tend to be organized by large corporations.

instruments of production: The tools and techniques used in the process of production.

Internationale: The anthem of the revolutionary working-class movement. Eugène Pottier, a member of the revolutionary Paris Commune of 1871, composed the anthem: "Arise, you prisoners of starvation!/ Arise, you wretched of the earth!/ For justice thunders condemnation:/ A better world's in birth!/ No more tradition's chains shall bind us,/ Arise you slaves, no more in thrall!/ The earth shall rise on new foundations:/ We have been nought, we shall be all!/ 'Tis the final conflict,/ Let each stand in his place./ The international soviet/ Shall be the human race./ 'Tis the final conflict,/ Let each stand in his place./ The international working class/ Shall be the human race."

kinship: The way in which people reckon their connections to each other through birth, adoption, and marriage. At one time kinship was the central focus of anthropological study. Today anthropologists still pay attention to kinship, but it is no longer the primary focus of anthropological research.

langoustine: Prawn-like spiny lobster of the genus *Nephrops*. Commonly called Norway prawn in English, langoustines are one of the most economically important seafoods harvested by Bigouden fishers.

longline: See entry under **fishing gear**.

Luddite: The term comes from a nineteenth-century British social movement of weavers who protested attacks on their working conditions by destroying mechanized looms. It has come to describe working-class movements and protests that identify machines and technological change as the primary cause of worsening conditions for workers.

mode of production: "A specific, historically occurring set of social relations through which labour is deployed to wrest energy from nature by means of tools, skills, organization, and knowledge" (Wolf 1982, 75).

modernization: The transition from a rural agrarian society to an industrial society. Modernization can be a description of a social transformation, a theoretical model of social transformation, or a political agenda designed to create economic development along capitalist lines. In this book modernization is used to describe the process of change that shifted rural Brittany from a primary agrarian economy into an industrial food-production region.

neo-liberal globalization: A form of economic globalization linked to a late twentieth-century/early twenty-first-century political agenda designed to weaken the authority of nation-states and to increase the flow of capital, goods, and services across national borders, while simultaneously limiting the mobility of labour.

peasants: Those who work under a form of agricultural production in which small tracts of land are owned and operated by families. While peasant agriculturalists often own their own land, their economic independence is often limited by local or regional elites. (See **simple commodity production**.)

prefect (prefecture): France is divided into administrative units called departments, which are similar to North American counties or townships. However, these administrative units are in essence a branch of the national government. The Prefecture is what the administrative arm of the national government at the department level is called. It has a fair degree of administrative and policing authority.

proletarianization: The process whereby people, classically peasants or tribal peoples, are transformed into wage labourers—people who own nothing but their own labour power, which they must sell to capitalists in order to live.

red flag: In the French context the red flag is both an international symbol of working-class struggle and a local reference to the French Republic's own history of revolution and reaction. It is directly embedded within France's national tri-colour flag of red (republic), white (the clergy and royalty), and blue (the bourgeoisie).

Révolte des Bonnets Rouges (Revolt of the Red Bonnets): The apocryphal moment of Bigouden history out of which is said to have emerged the unique lace coiffe of the region.

Sardine Years: The moment in Bigouden history in which the fishery for sardines was the primary fishery, 1860s–1930s. The period was noted for its militant labour politics. In the early 1900s the fishery faced a particularly severe crisis in which fish stocks were depleted. Poor living and working conditions exacerbated the economic impacts of the lack of fish.

seine: See entry under **fishing gear**.

share agreement (division of the catch): The way in which the proceeds of the fishing trip are divided among the vessel crew and boat owner. The typical system in the Bigouden fleet is to deduct the common charges (fuel, ice, food, taxes, etc.) from the gross revenue. The net amount is then divided between boat and crew, typically on a 50/50 basis.

simple commodity production: A unique set of relations of production, which are neither fully capitalist nor artisanal-based, but locked through market circuits to capital and through labour requirements to family. Thus, simple commodity producers are reliant upon a capitalist market place to sell their product (in this case fish) and to purchase the materials required to keep their operations functioning. However, they are also reliant upon various forms of family labour (including their own) for key operations of their enterprise. This allows a simple commodity producer to suppress the cost of labour relative to what they might otherwise have had to pay if they tried to purchase it on the labour market directly. In analytic terms simple commodity producers are similar to peasant agriculturalists. (See also **commodity**.)

social class: Two basic models of social class are used by social scientists. One divides people into groups based on common characteristics such as income, education, or occupation. The model of social class used in this book is relational: a person's relation to the means of production determines social class. For example, social class in the Bigouden fishery can be understood in terms of a class who owns boats and a class that works for the people who own the boats.

socially necessary labour time: The average quantity of labour, operating with the average skill, required to produce a commodity. Firms that cannot produce commodities at the minimum of socially necessary labour time typically fail. This is part of the dynamic that propels capitalist firms into expanded social reproduction.

social relations of production: The relationships people enter into in the process of production. Different types of societies use different ways of organizing people for production. For example, in kin-ordered societies kinship is used to organize the process of production. In a capitalist society labour for production is bought and sold on a theoretically free market.

social reproduction: How a society or social formation reproduces itself over time. In terms of basic units of production, such as a family-based fishing enterprise, one can talk of simple and expanded reproduction. Simple reproduction reproduces the enterprise without economic growth. Expanded reproduction involves the economic growth and expansion of the unit of production. Family-based enterprises, such as the Bigouden artisanal fishers, typically are involved in simple reproduction in order to allow for intergenerational transfer of the enterprise. Capitalist firms must typically engage in expanded reproduction or run the risk of bankruptcy.

strikes: See entry under **la grève**.

trap: See entry under **fishing gear**.

trawl: See entry under **fishing gear**.

trawlers (dragger): A type of fishing boat that uses trawl nets to harvest fish. This is the primary type of boat now fishing in the Bigoudennie. During the Sardine Years the typical fishboat was a sardine seiner.

World Forum of Fish Harvesters (WFF): An international alliance of artisanal fisher harvester organizations whose objective is to support and improve the condition of small-scale fishers globally.

REFERENCES

Acheson, James M. 1988. *The lobster gangs of Maine*. Hanover, NH: University Press of New England.

Adam, Paul. 1987. Les bouleversements des pêches contemporaines (1945–1985). In *Histoire des pêches maritimes en France*, ed. Michel Mollat. 297–320. Paris: Bibliothèque Historique Privat.

Ahmad, Aijaz. 1992. *In theory: Classes, nations, literatures*. London: Verso.

Allison, Charlene, Sue-Ellen Jacobs, and Mary A. Porter. 1989. *Winds of change: Women in Northwest commercial fishing*. Seattle: University of Washington Press.

Arbo, Peter, and Bjørn Hersoug. 1997. The globalization of the fishing industry and the case of Finnmark. *Marine Policy* 21(2): 121–42.

Badone, Ellen. 1989. *The appointed hour: Death, worldview, and social change in Brittany*. Berkeley: University of California Press.

———. 1992. The construction of national identity in Brittany and Quebec. *American Ethnologist* 19(4): 806–17.

Banaji, Jarius. 1977. Modes of production in a materialist conception of history. *Capital and Class* 3: 1–44.

Barrett, Michèle. 1980. *Women's oppression today: Problems in Marxist feminist analysis*. London: Verso.

Becker, Gay. 1997. *Disrupted lives: How people create meaning in a chaotic world*. Berkeley: University of California Press.

Beechey, Veronica. 1977. Women and production: A critical analysis of some sociological theories of women's work. *Capital and Class* 3: 45–66.

Benston, Margaret. 1969. The political economy of women's liberation. *Monthly Review* 21(4): 13–27.

Benton, Lauren. 1990. *Invisible factories: The informal economy and industrial development in Spain*. Albany: SUNY Press.

Best, Steven, and Douglas Kellner. 1991. *Postmodern theory: Critical interrogations*. New York: The Guilford Press.

Binkley, Marion. 1995. *Risks, dangers, and rewards in the Nova Scotia offshore fishery.* Montreal: McGill-Queen's University Press.

Blim, Michael. 1992. Introduction: The emerging global factory. In *Anthropology and the global factory: Studies of the new industrialization in the late twentieth century,* eds. Frances Rothstein and Michael Blim. 1–30. New York: Bergen & Garvey.

Bluestone, Barry, and Bennet Harrison. 1982. *The deindustrialization of America.* New York: Basic Books.

Borneman, John, and Abdellah Hammoudi, eds. 2009. *Being there: The fieldwork encounter and the making of truth.* Berkeley: University of California Press.

Boulard, Jean-Claude. 1991. *L'épopée de la Sardine: Un siècle d'histoires de pêches.* Paris: Éditions Ouest-France, IFREMER.

Bukharin, Nikolai. 1929. *Imperialism and world economy.* Moscow: Progress Publishers.

Butler, Caroline F. 2005. Fear fishing and speculation: The impacts of political knowledge on fishing practice. Unpublished paper presented at the Ocean Management Research Network Annual Conference. Ottawa. September 29–October 1, 2005.

Callinicos, Alex. 1989. *Against postmodernism: A Marxist critique.* Cambridge: Polity Press.

Chatain, Roland. 1994. *La pêche bigoudène: Histoire et évolution.* Plomeur: Éditions Roland CHATAIN.

Chaussade, Jean, and Jean-Pierre Corlay. 1988. *Atlas des pêches et des cultures marine en France.* Montpellier: RECLUS.

Clark, Margaret Elwyn. 1988. Managing uncertainty: Family, religion, and collective action among fishermen's wives in Gloucester, Massachusetts. In *To work and to weep: Women in fishing economies,* eds. Jane Nadel-Klein and Donna Lee Davis. St. John's: ISER, Memorial University of Newfoundland.

Cleac'h, Annick, and Nicole Piriou. 1993. Le sud du Pays Bigouden: De la crise agricole à la maritimité triomphante." In *Le Pays Bigouden à la croisée des chemins,* ed. Nicole Piriou. 335–43. Pont L'Abbé: Cap Caval.

Clement, Wallace. 1986. *The struggle to organize: Resistance in Canada's fishery.* Toronto: McClelland & Stewart.

Cliff, Tony. 1988. *State capitalism in Russia.* London: Bookmarks.

Cohen, A.P. 1987. *Whalsay: Symbol, segment, and boundary in a Shetland Island community.* Manchester: Manchester University Press.

Cole, Sally C. 1991. *Women of the praia: Work and lives in a Portuguese coastal community.* Princeton, NJ: Princeton University Press.

Cornou, Jakez. 1993. *La coiffe bigoudène: Histoire d'une étrange parure.* Pont L'Abbé: SKED.

Couliou, Jean-René. 1994. "Les manifestations de marins pêcheurs en 1993 et 1994" and "Les actions des marins pêcheurs du Grand-Ouest en 1993." *Atlas permanent de la mer et du littoral* 1: 11–12.

Cousiné-Kervennic, Noëlle. 1994. *Le Pays Bigouden*. Rennes: Éditions Ouest-France.

Day, Frank Parker. 1928 (1989). *Rockbound*. Toronto: University of Toronto Press.

Dobbin, Frank. 1994. *Forging industrial policy: The United States, Britain, and France in the railway age*. Cambridge: Cambridge University Press.

Dorval, Patrick. 1987. *Sécurité et conditions de travail à la pêche artisanale et semi industrielle*. Paris: Institut Français de Recherche pour l'Exploitation de la Mer.

Duigou, Serge. 1989. *La révolte des bonnets rouges en Pays Bigouden*. Quimper: Éditions · RESSAC.

———. 1990. *Les bigoudens (et surtout les bigoudènes)*. Quimper: Éditions RESSAC.

———. 1991. *Quand les bigoudens sillonnaient les mers*. Quimper: Éditions RESSAC.

———. 1994. *Les mystères de Penmarc'h*. Quimper: Éditions RESSAC.

Fairley, Bryant O. 1985. The struggle for capitalism in the fishing industry in Newfoundland. *Studies in Political Economy* 17: 33–69.

Farnell, John, and James Elles. 1984. *In search of a common fisheries policy*. Aldershot, UK: Gower Publishing Company.

Fields, Leslie Leyland. 1997. *The entangling net: Alaska's commercial fishing women tell their lives*. Urbana, IL: University of Illinois Press.

Forest, John. 1988. *Lord I'm coming home: Everyday aesthetics in Tidewater North Carolina*. Ithaca, NY: Cornell University Press.

Friedmann, Harriet. 1978. Simple commodity production and wage labor in the American Plains. *Journal of Peasant Studies* 6(1): 71–100.

———. 1980. Household production and the national economy: Concepts for the analysis of agrarian formations. *Journal of Peasant Studies* 7(2): 158–84.

Geertz, Clifford. 1988. *Works and lives: The anthropologist as author*. Stanford, CA: Stanford University Press.

Gough, Ian. 1979. *The political economy of the welfare state*. London: MacMillan.

Guégruen, Michel, and Louis-Pierre Le Maitre. 1990. *Matelots de Concarneau (1800–1914)*. Concarneau, self-published.

Guppy, Neil. 1987. Labouring at sea: Harvesting an uncommon property. In *Uncommon property: The fishing and fish-processing industries in British Columbia*, eds. Patricia Marchak, Neil Guppy, and John McMullan. 173–98. Toronto: Methuen.

Gwiazda, Adam. 1993. The Common Fisheries Policy: Economic aspects. *Marine Policy* 17(4): 251–55.

Habermas, Jürgen. 1986. *Autonomy and solidarity: Interviews with Jürgen Habermas*. Ed. Peter Dews. London: Verso.

Harman, Chris. 1991. The state and capitalism today. *International Socialism* 51: 3–54.

Harvey, David. 1989. *The condition of postmodernity: An enquiry into the origins of cultural change*. Oxford: Blackwell.

Hélias, Pierre-Jakez. 1978. *The horse of pride: Life in a Breton village*. New Haven, CT: Yale University Press.

Hemingway, Ernest. 1952. *The old man and the sea*. New York: Scribner.

Hobsbawm, E.J. 1969. *Industry and empire*. Harmondsworth: Penguin Books.

Holden, Mike. 1994. *The Common Fisheries Policy: Origin, evaluation, and future.* Oxford: Fishing News Books.

Jensen, Vickie. 1995. *Saltwater women at work.* Vancouver: Douglas & McIntyre.

Lachèvre, Yvon. 1994. *La sardine: Toute une histoire.* Quimper: Patrimoine Maritime.

Laclau, Ernesto, and Chantal Mouffe. 1985. *Hegemony and socialist strategy: Towards a radical democratic politics.* London: Verso.

Le Bail, Joël, and Claude Nicot. 1995. Le modèle halieutique Bigouden a l'épreuve de la crise. *Revue Norois* 167: 499–515.

Lebel, Anne. 1981. Les luttes sociales dans la conserverie et le milieu maritime, en 1926 et 1927, sur le littoral Bigouden. MA thesis. Brest: Université de Bretagne Occidentale.

Le Coadic, Ronan. 2003. Les contrastes Bretons. *Ethnologie française* 33(3): 373–79.

Le Coz, Bruno. 1985. La crise sardinière au Pays Bigouden maritime, 1902–1908. MA thesis. Brest: Université de Bretagne Occidentale.

Lehning, James R. 1995. *Peasant and French: Cultural contact in rural France during the nineteenth century.* Cambridge: Cambridge University Press.

Leigh, Michael. 1983. *European integration and the Common Fisheries Policy.* London and Canberra: Croom Helm.

Lenin, Vladimir. 1934. *Imperialism, the highest stage of capitalism.* Moscow: Progress Publishers.

Lévi-Strauss, Claude. 1974. *Triste tropiques.* New York: Atheneum.

Lévy-Leboyer, Maurice, and François Bourguignon. 1990. *The French economy in the nineteenth century: An essay in econometric analysis.* Trans. Jesse Bryant and Virginie Pérotin. Cambridge: Cambridge University Press.

Le Wita, Beatrix. 1994. *French bourgeois culture.* Trans. J.A. Underwood. Cambridge: Cambridge University Press.

LiPuma, Edward, and Sarah Keene Meltzoff. 1994. Economic mediation and the power of associations: Toward a concept of encompassment. *American Anthropologist* 96(1): 31–51.

Luke, Timothy W. 1989. Class contradictions and social cleavages in informationalizing post-industrial societies: On the rise of new social movements. *New Political Science* 6(17): 125–55.

Magraw, Roger. 1983. *France 1814–1915: The bourgeois century.* London: Fontana.

———. 1992. *A history of the French working class.* Oxford: Blackwell.

Marchak, Patricia. 1984. Introduction: Special issue on fisheries. *Journal of Canadian Studies* 19(1): 1–10.

Martin, Anne-Denes. 1994. *Les ouvrières de la mer: Histoire des sardinières du littoral Breton.* Paris: L'Harmattan.

Marx, Karl, and Fredrick Engels. 1969. *Selected works in three volumes: Volume one.* Moscow: Progress Publishers.

McDonald, Maryon. 1989. *"We are not French!" Language, culture, and identity in Brittany.* London: Routledge.

Mead, Margaret. 1935. *Sex and temperament in three primitive societies.* New York: New American Library.

Menzies, Charles R. 1990. Between the stateroom and the fo'c'sle: Everyday forms of class struggle aboard a commercial fishboat. *Nexus* 8(1): 77–92.

———. 1991. Obscenities and fisher*men:* The (re)production of gender in the process of production. *Anthropology of Work Review* 12(2): 13–16.

———. 1992. On permanent strike: Class and ideology in a producers' co-operative. *Studies in Political Economy* 38: 85–108.

———. 1993. All that holds us together: Kinship and resource pooling in a fishing co-operative. MAST: *Maritime Anthropological Studies* 6(1/2): 157–79.

———. 1997. Class and identity on the margins of industrial society: A Breton illustration. *Anthropologica* 39: 27–38.

———. 2002. Red flags and lace coiffes: Identity, livelihood, and the politics of survival in the Bigoudennie, France. In *Culture, economy, power: Anthropology as critique, anthropology as praxis*, eds. Winnie Lem and Belinda Leach. 235–49. Albany: SUNY Press.

———. 2003. Fishing, families, and the survival of artisanal boat-ownership in the Bigouden Region of France. MAST, *Maritime Studies* 2(1): 71–88.

Menzies, Charles R., and Jennifer Rashleigh. 2008. *Face à la tempête/Weather the Storm*. Bullfrog Films.

Morin, Edgar. 1967. *La métamorphose de Plozevet: Commune en France*. Paris: Fayard.

Nadel-Klein, Jane, and Donna Lee Davis. 1988. *To work and to weep: Women in fishing economies*. St. John's: ISER, Memorial University of Newfoundland.

Noiriel, Gérard. 1990. *Workers in French society in the 19th and 20th centuries*. Trans. Helen McPhail. New York: Berg.

Ortner, Sherry. 1974. Is female to male as nature is to culture? In *Women, culture, & society*, eds. Michelle Zimbalist Rosaldo and Louise Lamphere. 67–88. Stanford, CA: Stanford University Press.

Palmer, Bryan D. 1990. *Descent into discourse: The reification of language and the writing of social science*. Philadelphia: Temple University Press.

———. 1992. *Working class experience: Rethinking the history of Canadian labour, 1800–1991*. Toronto: McClelland & Stewart.

———. 1994. *Capitalism comes to the backcountry: The Goodyear invasion of Napanee*. Toronto: Between the Lines.

Rogers, Raymond A. 1995. *The oceans are emptying: Fish wars and sustainability*. Montreal: Black Rose Books.

Sabean, David Warren. 1984. *Power in the blood: Popular culture and village discourse in early modern Germany*. Cambridge: Cambridge University Press.

Salz, Pavel. 1991. *The European Atlantic fisheries: Structure, economic performance, and policy*. The Hague: Agricultural Economics Research Institute (LEI-DLO).

Secombe, Wally. 1974. The housewife and her labor under capitalism. *New Left Review* 83: 3–24.

Segalen, Martine. 1984. Avoir sa part: Sibling relations in partible inheritance Brittany. In *Interest and emotion: Essays on the study of family and kinship*, eds. Hans Medick and David Warren Sabean. 129–44. Cambridge: Cambridge University Press.

———. 1991. *Fifteen generations of Bretons: Kinship and society in lower Brittany, 1720–1980.* Cambridge: Cambridge University Press.

Sider, Gerald M. 1996. Cleansing history: Lawrence, Massachusetts, the strike for four loaves of bread and no roses, and the anthropology of working-class consciousness. *Radical Review of History* 65: 48–83.

———. 1997a. Against experience. In *Between history and histories: The making of silences and commemorations*, eds. Gerald Sider and Gavin Smith. Toronto: University of Toronto Press.

———. 1997b. The making of peculiar local cultures: Producing and surviving history in peasant and tribal societies. In *Was bleibt von marxistischen perspektiven in der geschichtsforschung?*, ed. Alf Lüdtke. 101–48. Götingen: Wallstein Verlag.

———. 2003. *Between history and tomorrow: Making and breaking everyday life in rural Newfoundland.* Peterborough, ON: Broadview Press.

Sinclair, Peter R. 1985. *From traps to draggers: Domestic commodity production in Northwest Newfoundland, 1950–1982.* St. John's: ISER, Memorial University of NFLD.

Smith, Gavin. 1989. *Livelihood and resistance: Peasants and the politics of land in Peru.* Berkeley: University of California Press.

———. 1991. Writing for real: Capitalist constructions and constructions of capitalism. *Critique of Anthropology* 11(3): 213–32.

Smith, M. Estellie. 1988. The right to choice: Power and decision making. In *To work and to weep: Women in fishing economies*, eds. Jane Nadel-Klein and Donna Lee Davis. 279–92. St. John's: ISER, Memorial University of Newfoundland.

Stark, David. 1980. Class struggle and the transformation of the labour process: A relational approach. *Theory and Society* 9(1): 89–130.

Stump, Ken, and Dave Batker. 1996. *Sinking fast: How factory trawlers are destroying US fisheries and marine ecosystems.* Washington, DC: Greenpeace.

Teeple, Gary. 1995. *Globalization and the decline of social reform.* Toronto: Garamond Press.

Thompson, E.P. 1963. *The making of the English working class.* Harmondsworth: Penguin Books.

Tillon, Charles. 1977. *On chantait rouge.* Paris: Éditions Robert Laffont.

Vauclare, Claude. 1985. *Les pêches maritimes en Pays Bigouden: Matériaux pour une contribution à l'histoire socio-économique des pêches.* Paris: IFREMER, CEASM.

———. 1987. Naissance d'une industrie. In *Histoire des pêches maritimes en France*, ed. Michel Mollat. 243–97. Paris: Bibliothèque Historique Privat.

Vogel, Lise. 1983. *Marxism and the oppression of women: Toward a unitary theory.* New Brunswick, NJ: Rutgers University Press.

Walker, Spike. 1988. The agony and the ecstasy of a seven day halibut season. *National Fisherman* 68: 13.

Weber, Eugen. 1976. *Peasants into Frenchmen: The modernization of rural France, 1870–1914.* Stanford, CA: Stanford University Press.

Wise, Mark. 1984. *The Common Fisheries Policy of the European Community.* London: Methuen.

Wolf, Eric R. 1966. *Peasants*. Englewood Cliffs, NJ: Prentice-Hall.

———. 1982. *Europe and the people without history*. Berkeley: University of California Press.

Wood, Ellen Meiksins. 1996. Modernity, postmodernity, or capitalism? *Monthly Review* 48(3): 21–39.

Worsley, Peter. 1984. *The three worlds: Culture and world development*. London: Weidenfeld and Nicolson.

INDEX